Old Grandpa's Songbook

Volume 2: Love Songs

Music and Lyrics
by David G. Lanoue

Old Grandpa's Songbook: Volume 2, Love Songs

Music and Lyrics by David G. Lanoue

ISBN: 978-1-7333016-4-0
New Orleans, HaikuGuy.com

Old Grandpa's Songbook

Volume 2: Love Songs

for you who let me love you

Table of Contents

Moonlight Sonata

```
G          Am            Em  G       Am          A7
here is my moonlight sonata that I am playing for you
D                        Em    D                        G
though I was never your lover, will you bear with me, I want to please?
    G            Am          Em
the moon on your face and the water just now
G          Am         A7
made me remember a woman like you
C7         D7           Em    C7         D7       Em
no, I won't bore you with details, will you sit with me a while?
Em                     Em           A7
moonlit your face when I met you just now
   A7          B7          Em
it took me to summers gone by
Em                        C7   Am       B7      Em
am I that older that different today? am I that wiser to say?
```

→ [here is my . . .]

```
Em  G   B7              C7    B7          Em
like the moon, it will pass soon, it will pass soon
```

Moonlight Sonata

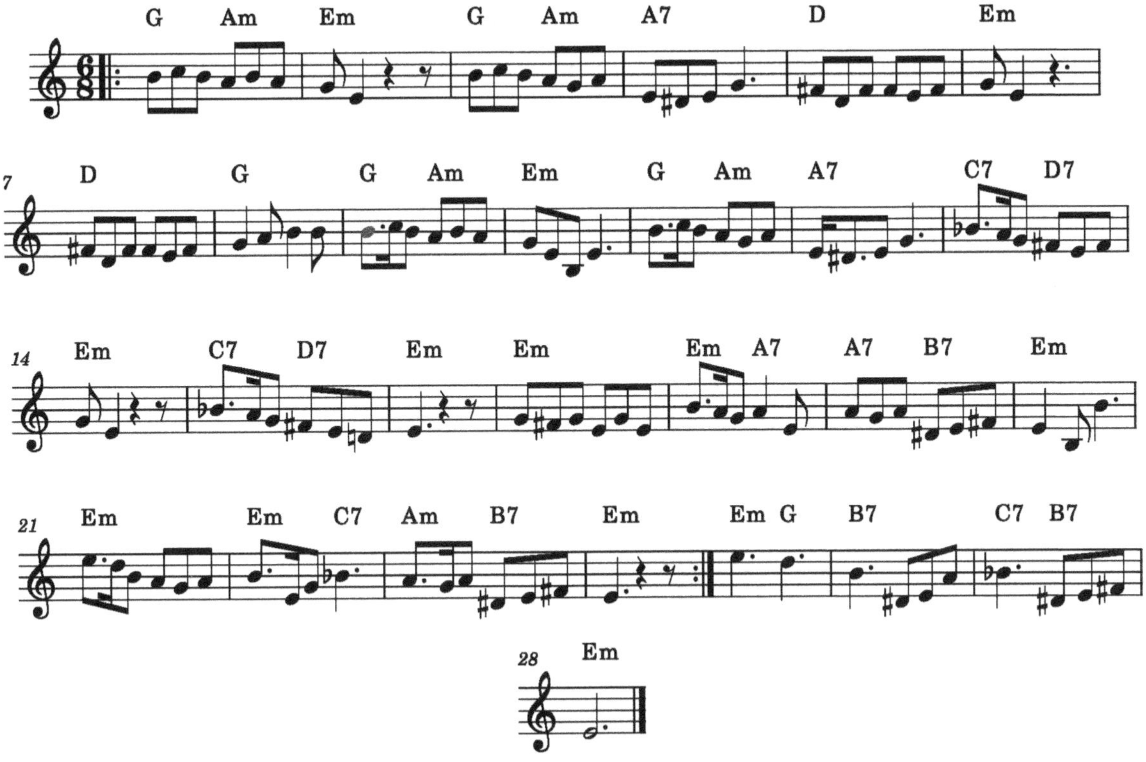

Sailboat

```
Em              Bm        F#7              Bm
have you seen a sailboat, light and pretty sailboat?
Em            Bm          F#7
I have been watching here
D                  A7         F#7          Bm
waiting for my sailboat, easy breezy sailboat
Em                 Bm F#7      Bm
have you seen a sailboat?
```

```
Em              Bm        F#7              Bm
she is like a sailboat, lifts me on the ocean
Em            Bm         F#7
sails me away so I'm
D                  A7          F#7              Bm
waiting for my sailboat to take me from this madness
Em                 Bm F#7      Bm
have you seen a sailboat?
```

```
D                  A7          F#7          Bm
do do do do, do do do do, do do do do, do do do do
Em       Bm              F#7    Bm
do do, do do do do, do
```

```
Em                 Bm      F#7              Bm
such a vast, vast ocean people can get lost on
Em            Bm                F#7
sailing in an endless aimless breeze
D                  A7         F#7              Bm
have you seen a sailboat, light and pretty sailboat
 Em            Bm        F#7    Bm
do you think she's forgotten me?
```

Sailboat

© 1973 David G. Lanoue

Café du Monde

```
       G            D          Cma9  G
you ask me why I stare in Café du Monde
      Cma9                 G
my eyes have found a home
             D       D7
and they're resting there,
G          D          Cma9        G
thank you, thank you for being on that bus
      Cma9   G         D          D7
the two of us on the Carrollton bus


       G         D        Cma9         G
I'm sitting in my room looking at the phone
Cma9            G         D       D7
thinking of that poem that I gave to you
G          D          Cma9            G
thank you, thank you for wanting to know me
      Cma9               G
for telling me your street
            D        D7     G
and I'm going to see . . . you
```

Café du Monde

Naoko

```
Fma9   Cma9              D7
hello, my friend in Japan
          Cma9              D7
miss your voice, miss your hands
        Fma9        D7
understand if you can
Fma9   Cma9          D7        C   Fma9   C   D7
we are far apart but close, Naoko

Fma9     Cma9              D7
no one knows how hard it is
          Cma9              D7
at the graves I wanted your kiss
             Fma9        D7
and I'm not sorry for the wish
Fma9     Cma9              D7        C   Fma9   C   D7
no one knows you like I know, Naoko

Fma9       Cma9              D7
love songs don't amount to much
          Cma9        D7
without smile, without touch
             Fma9        D7
it seems such a sad waste
Fma9   Cma9              D7        C   Fma9   C
but I'll sing this till you know, Naoko
```

Naoko

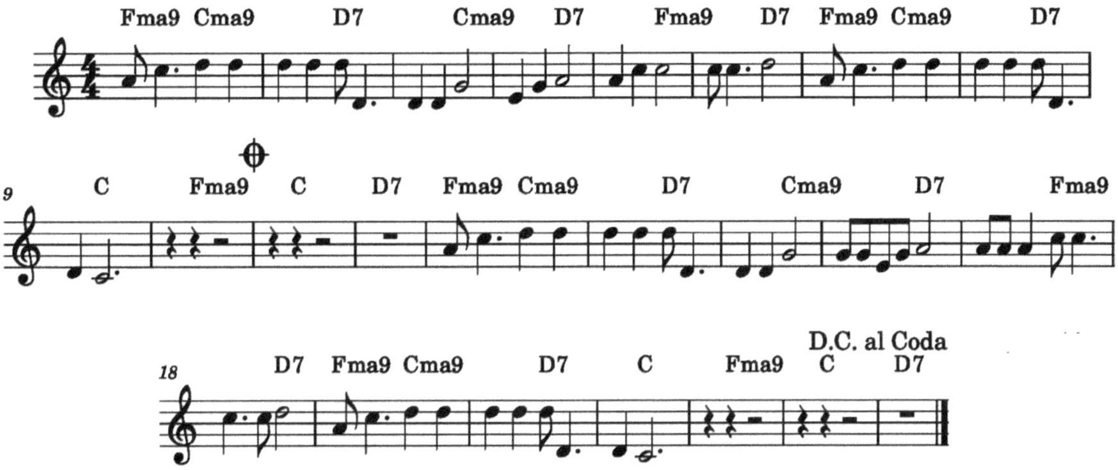

Carmen

```
C  C+   F        Fm6 C    C  C+   F        Fm6    C
```
Carmen, here we go again, so slow putting on our clothes
```
C  F+    Bb    Bbm6 Fm6       C
```
Carmen, I really need a friend, Carmen

```
C  C+ F      Fm6     C     C     C+ F            Fm6   C
```
I spy sassy dazzling eyes, zoom in, there's that smile again
```
C  F+    Bb         Bbm6   Fm6     C
```
Carmen, please, it's not the end, Carmen

```
C   C+   F         Fm6 C    C  C+       F       Fm6   C
```
Carmen starts her car again, we kiss, she drives into the mist
```
C   F+    Bb          Bbm6 Fm6     C
```
Carmen, I know this is the end, Carmen

Carmen

Janae on the Treadmill

```
A E          A    E
Janae on the treadmill
       D      Ama6  E7    A    E
in the fitness center on the fifth floor
A E          A   E              D    Ama6  E7       A E
I  say, you go fast girl, she says not as fast as I've gone before


A  E          A     E
so I start to bench press
            D       Ama6     E7      A  E
while she's running hard but going nowhere
A E          A    E
I  try hard to impress
         D      Ama6   E7       A E
but she doesn't notice the way I stare


E               Ama6  D7  E
on the treadmill how she glides
E            Ama6  D7 E
beautiful girl, just my type


A  E               A  E
my heart goes pitter pat
    D      Ama6    E7          A E
as I try to think of something to say
A  E            A    E
I'm starting to feel fat
     D       Ama6   E7        A E
as I compare myself to sweet Janae


E               Ama6  D7  E
on the treadmill how she glides
E            Ama6  D7 E
beautiful girl, just my type
```

Janae on the Treadmill

© 1997 David G. Lanoue

Barbie

```
G              Gdim           D           Ddim
```
G. I. Joe can't take his eyes off Barbie in her hot pink car
```
Gm             Bm             Dm          G7
```
how he longs to hold her in his kung fu grip so tight
```
Bb         Gdim            F           Ddim
```
Barbie doesn't notice him, she's wishing on a twinkling star
```
Bbm        Dm             Fm                 Bb7   G
```
seeing herself far away, she's gliding off into the night, Barbie

```
G              Gdim           D           Ddim
```
G. I. Joe, the lonely fool rappelling from the ceiling fan
```
Gm             Bm             Dm          G7
```
all his manly muscles bulging, yelling, "Look at me!"
```
Bb         Gdim                F           Ddim
```
Barbie in her dreamhouse dreaming maybe Europe or Japan
```
Bbm        Dm             Fm                         Bb7   G
```
far beyond this dusty toy room, somewhere where she can be free, Barbie

```
G              Gdim           D           Ddim
```
ten years later Joe's a vet, he drives a truck for Amazon
```
Gm             Bm             Dm          G7
```
on his dashboard Barbie's picture smiles at him, so sweet
```
Bb         Gdim         F           Ddim
```
Barbie moved to Italy, she's selling candles in Milan
```
Bbm    Dm             Fm              Bb7  G
```
not a C.E.O., not rich but plenty of pasta to eat, Barbie

Barbie

Confusing Girl

```
E          Am            E     Am
she wants a house filled with seven dogs
E          Am            E       Am E         Am Dm6        E
out in the country in the pea soup fog, she wants to fly around the  world
E          Am        Dm6         C
she wants a baby to spoil like none other
E          Am          Dm6 C      E      Am  Dm6      E
she says she never wants to be a mother, she is a very  confusing girl
Ama7                            Gma6
she wants a four-carat diamond ring, she says she don't want anything
Cma7    D7        E
she is a confusing girl


E          Am         E    Am
she wants to work on a reservation
E          Am      E   Am  E         Am        Dm6       E
wants to continue her education, she wants to dance and glide and whirl
E          Am            Dm6 C      E
she wants commitment and to say I do, a Mercedes
Am          Dm6      C    E      Am Dm6       E
station wagon painted blue, she is a very confusing girl
Ama7                          Gma6
she says she wants to live with me, she says she needs her liberty
Cma7    D7         E
she is a confusing girl


E           Am           E     Am
she wants the two of us to settle down
E           Am      E    Am  E         Am        Dm6       E
she wants to party and run around, she wants to marry the Duke of Earl
E         Am           Dm6    C
she says money don't mean a thing
E          Am          Dm6       C   E      Am Dm6       E
she wants a four-carat diamond ring, she is a very confusing girl
Ama7                            Gma6
she says she wants me for her man, she says she only wants in my pants
Cma7    D7         E
she is a confusing girl
```

Confusing Girl

23

What Lovers Do

```
D#                    Gm
I am in love with you
D#                    Fm
I can't control the storm
G#              G#dim
I am the storm, I'll die for you
D#
that's what lovers do
G       Bm
God is dreaming
G       Am
us because
C               Cdim   G
that's what lovers do


D#                    Gm
I held my father's hand
D#                    Fm
I don't know if he heard
G#                  G#dim
so many words I had to spew
D#
that's what lovers do
G       Bm
he' s in heaven
G       Am
let's pretend
C               Cdim   G
that's what lovers do
```

What Lovers Do

Dewdrop World

```
Dm              C        Dm              Dm6 C      Dm
this world is a dewdrop world, things pass, no nothing lasts
Dm          C     Dm
a boy and a little girl
      F    E7        F   E7        F   E7   Dm
on a dewdrop, tiny dewdrop, it's a dewdrop world


Dm                C         Dm             Dm6 C      Dm
he loves how she looks at him, she loves his shining skin
Dm              C         Dm
hot sun burns away the pearls
      F    E7        F   E7          F   E7   Dm
of the dewdrops, tiny dewdrops, it's a dewdrop world


Dm              C         Dm             Dm6 C     Dm
a ring made of hard cool stone, tells her she's not alone
Dm              C           Dm
they watch lazy smoke rings curl
      F   E7          F   E7          F   E7   Dm      Dm  C  Dm
on a dewdrop, that they can't stop, fading dewdrop world
```

Dewdrop World

© 1990 David G. Lanoue

I Got Some Last Night

```
E                         Cma7            E           G
morning look at me with a smile on my face, I can't erase, no way
E                                 Cma7              E         G
we wake up together though it's been far too long, last night baby stayed

  E           Cma9   E            A
I got some last night, I cleaned out my pipes
        E        G       E
now my world feels just right, just right

E                         Cma7            E                 G
saw her at her sisters, we ate birthday cake, I couldn't mistake that look
E                               Cma7            E
driving down the dark highway, hands I know so well touched me
     G
and I shook

  E           Cma9   E            A
I got some last night, I cleaned out my pipes
        E        G       E
now my world feels just right, just right

E                         Cma7            E                 G
morning look at her with a smile on her face, she searches for her clothes
E                         Cma7            E           G
I ask her to stay but she tells me no way, we lost that long ago

        E           Cma9     E              A
she just got some last night, she cleaned out her pipes
        E        G       E
now her world feels just right, just right
```

I Got Some Last Night

© 1990 David G. Lanoue

Chemical Attraction

```
 Cm          D7      Bb          C7
I didn't love you until I learned how to
Em              F#7
now it seems so strange
D                   E7
love has changed us
Cm          D7      Bb          C7
is it chemical, this need I feel for you?
Em        F#7
I didn't love you
D      E7
now I do


G               A7
chemical attraction, it just
E       F#7           C#
can't explain what I feel
G                         F#7                E
something else was going on when suddenly
A7              G
love became real


 Cm          D7      Bb          C7
I didn't love you until my heart let me
Em          F#7
only love set me
D                           E7      B
free, this can't be just chemistry
```

Chemical Attraction

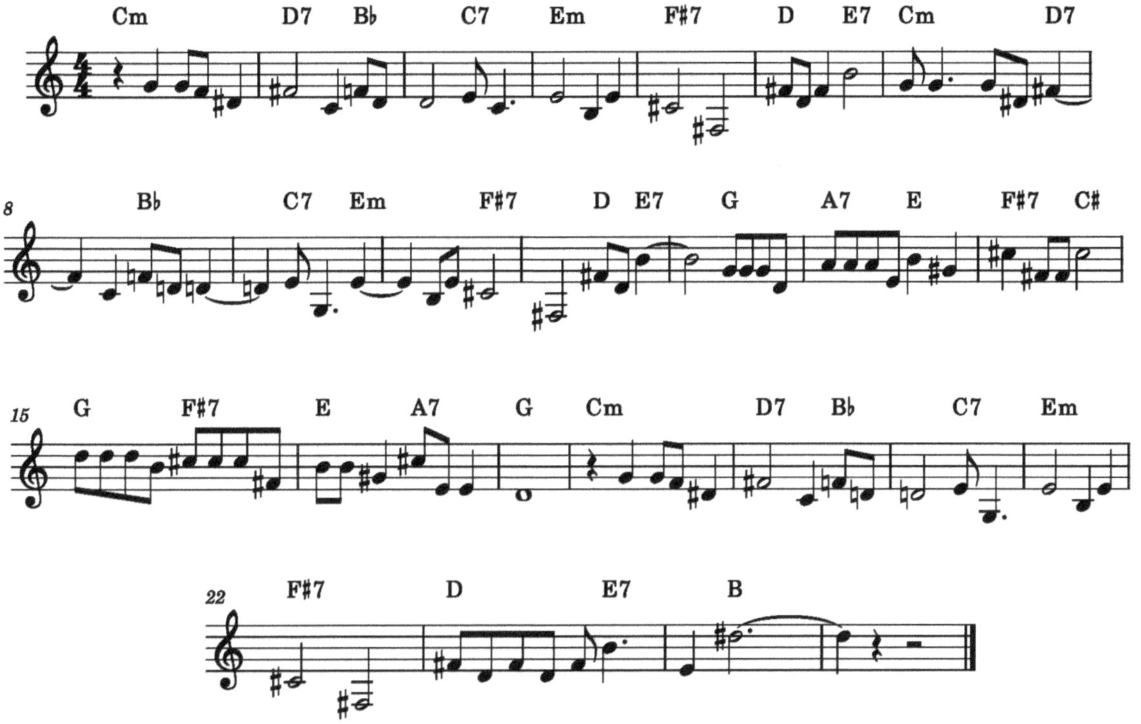

Not Your Man

```
D           Ddim
it's all over, thank you for your time,
G                                D
there are plans we should not plan
D           Ddim
like the raincloud, she lets down her hair,
G                       Dma9
dark and lovely on the land
G           Dma9 G      D
wherever she can, I'm not your man


D           Ddim
I love rivers, flowing old and deep
G                       D
better than the solid land
D           Ddim
I'm a drifter, and I've found you see
G                               Dma9
there are streams we should not dam
G                       Dma9  G     D
let them flow where they can,  I'm not your man


D     Ddim       Dma9   G7
like a raincloud letting go
D     Ddim  G     Dma9
like a river let it flow
G     Dma9 G      D
let it flow, let it go
```

Not Your Man

© 1982 David G. Lanoue

These Dreams

```
  A               Fma7    A            Gma6
I heard you on the phone, I listened to you breathe
  A               Fma7       A         G          A
I think he was at home, he was home, was he home? these dreams
   A              Fma7    A            Gma6
I saw you on the bus, you moved like a machine
           A              Fma7       A      G        A
there's no one left to trust, but we must, we must, these dreams


A        Fma7    Gma6  D   A  Fma7      G
though I lost you years ago, oh oh these dreams
  A         Fma7 Gma6   D   A   Fma7 G           A
I can't forget, I can't let go, oh oh it seems, these dreams


A               Fma7    A            Gma6
we were in the sky on tottering moon beams
  A                 Fma7        A        G          A
I feared we were too high, we were high, were we high? these dreams
  A             Fma7  A            Gma6
I held you on the stairs but your bright lips screamed
        A                 Fma7       A          G          A
and then you looked so scared, he was there, was he there? these dreams


A        Fma7    Gma6  D   A  Fma7      G
though I lost you years ago, oh oh these dreams
  A         Fma7 Gma6   D   A   Fma7 G           A
I can't forget,   I can't let go, oh oh it seems, these dreams
```

These Dreams

© 1986 David G. Lanoue

So Sweet Your Heartbeat

```
Fma7        C       Cma7      G      G7
ear to your chest, I hear the drum-drum
Fma7        E       Ema7   B     B7
my favorite tune, I hum, I hum-hum
D  Dma7          A      A7
so sweet your heartbeat
D         Dma7    A
it plays on and on
C               Cma7          G        G7
so sweet your heartbeat till you are gone
```

```
Fma7        C       Cma7      G    G7
the softest flute, I hear you sigh, I
Fma7        E       Ema7   B    B7
will dare to bet, it's saying not yet
D  Dma7          A      A7
no death, says your breath
D         Dma7    A
it sings on and on
C               Cma7             G         G7 C
no death says your breath till you are all gone
```

So Sweet Your Heartbeat

© 2023 David G. Lanoue

Three Girlfriends

```
        A              D7   A
I have three girlfriends . . . tonight
Em6           D            A
three girlfriends . . . what a lovely sight

Em6                      D7
I take them out to lunch, we giggle flirt and munch
            A
what a happy bunch we are → [I have . . .]

Em6                      D7
one is tall and blonde, we daydream by the pond
            A
and she is fond of me → [I have . . .]

Em6                      D7
one is short and black, says she has my back
            A
and she likes daiquiris → [I have . . .]

Em6                      D7
one has Spanish eyes, she collects butterflies
            A
and she buys ties for me → [I have . . .]

Em6                      D7
in bed we cuddle close, we kiss like Eskimos
            A
we wiggle our toes with glee → [I have . . .]
```

Three Girlfriends

© 1997 David G. Lanoue

Monday before Mardi Gras

```
G                              Dm
Monday before Mardi Gras, sitting by a window
C                              G
a bird sings better than I can
G                              Dm
I'm no one's valentine, not a moonstruck lover
C                        D      D#
today I'm only what I am, I am

G                              Dm
chomping an apple down, playing with my music
C                              G
she was sweet down to the core
G                              Dm
I'm no one's diplomat, I can't hide my feelings
C                              D      D#
I miss her much more than before, before

F              G            D
Monday morning without a fantasy to release me
F              G            Dm
maybe I need her, maybe I need her still
              C          G
need her still, need her still

G                      Dm
I'm lying in my teeth, thinking of a river
C                         G
I wonder just how deep it flows
G                    Dm
I may never know, she has dreams to finish
C                       D     D#
she has visions yet to sow, oh . . . → [Monday morning . . .]
```

Monday before Mardi Gras

© 1983 David G. Lanoue

Amen!

```
Cm          Bb           Cm             G7
I pray that you will be always right here
Dm           C                Dm          A7
too bad this prayer won't be answered, I fear
G         D
my sweet friend


Dm       C            Dm     A7
is it so wrong of us, is it a sin
Em              D              Em           B7
to know the deck is stacked, no one will win
A        E
in the end?


Am          G            Am             E7
there is no puffy cloud waiting for us
Bm             A              Bm         F#7
there are no harp-playing angels, I trust
E        B
forget them


Bm            A              Bm           F#7
but here we are right now, drunken on love
C#m               B            C#m          G#7
we don't need puffy white clouds up above
F# C#
amen!
```

Amen!

Esoterica

```
  G             D
adoring you is good for me and
      Am        C        G
and good for America as well
D         A       Em    G       D
kissing you keeps me off the road to hell


G             D
holding you saves me
      Am        C              G
without you my king, he stays in check
D             A       Em      G            D
your bewitching smile, I love every freckle on your neck

A               D             A
good for me and good for America
Am        G     D
I adore you Esoterica

G             D
better late than never
      Am        C          G
so happy to have found you, girlfriend
D         A       Em    G         D
I'll hold you tightly, until our journey's end

A               D             A
good for me and good for America
Am        G     D
I adore you Esoterica
```

Esoterica

St. Philip Street

G   Fma9   G
on St. Philip Street walking down by the school
Fma9   G   Fma9   G
looking in your eyes for you on St. Philip Street
G   Cma9   G
see . . . here's where we're meant to be
Cma9   G   Fma9   G
right where we're standing, see . . . on St. Philip Street

G   Fma9   G
I don't know you well but I love your soft, soft eyes
Fma9   G   Fma9   G
feel I've known you all my life, and St. Philip Street
G   Cma9   G
we . . . wander and at times we meet
Cma9   G   Fma9   G
underneath the branching trees . . . on St. Philip Street

G   Fma9   G
on St. Philip Street shadows in the balconies
Fma9   G   Fma9   G
looking in your eyes at peace on St. Philip Street
G   Cma9   G
see . . . here's where we're meant to be
Cma9   G   Fma9   G
right where we're standing, see . . . on St. Philip Street

G   Fma9   G
I tell you goodbye and I watch you walk away
Fma9   G   Fma9   G
off into the darkening day on St. Philip Street
G   Cma9   G
we . . . might meet again you see
  Cma9   G   Fma9   G
in new disguises we'll be . . . on St. Philip Street
Fma9   G   Fma9   G
on St. Philip Street . . . on St. Philip Street

St. Philip Street

© 1983 David G. Lanoue

Lost in Ikebukuro

```
E7    Ama7  D            A            E
I was lost in Ikebukuro, didn't have a clue
Ama7                     D        A        E7
what was the name of my hotel? I wished I knew
          Ama7  D        A        E
but I was lost in Ikebukuro, wandering around
Ama7           D         A      E7
neon signs in Japanese, a million sounds
E7    D    G    F#7      Fma7    E7
I was lost, lost, lost . . . in Ikebukuro
```

```
         Ama7          D         A            E
tried to call you from Ikebukuro, couldn't quite explain
Ama7                 D                    A        E7
you weren't home, I dropped the phone, it started to rain
          Ama7  D          A        E
and I was lost in Ikebukuro, felt so alone
Ama7           D            A            E7
all my bags in that old room, a long way from home
E7    D    G    F#7      Fma7    E7
I was lost, lost, lost . . . in Ikebukuro
```

```
E7  Ama7           D         A        E
the world is like Ikebukuro's mysterious streets
Ama7                     D                      A        E7
what's 'round that corner? we don't know, but we're dying to see
E7    D    G    F#7      Fma7    E7
I was lost, lost, lost . . . in Ikebukuro
E7    Ama7
I was lost
```

Lost in Ikebukuro

© 1987 David G. Lanoue

Blackout Night

```
D        Gma7      D          Gma7
```
blackout night, we read by flashlight
```
Am           D7        Am     D7
```
you and I, we sit together side by side, on
```
G      Cma7    G      Cma7
```
blackout night, it feels just right
```
Dm           G7
```
you and I, we eat the cashews
```
Dm              G7      C
```
till the lights come on, on blackout night

```
D        Gma7    D      Gma7
```
building's dark like Noah's ark
```
Am           D7            Am     D7
```
you and I, we laugh together, what a lark, it's
```
G      Cma7   G      Cma7
```
blackout time, it feels so fine
```
Dm           G7
```
you and I, we guzzle red wine
```
Dm              G7          C
```
till the lights all shine, don't shine yet, lights
```
C          G7      C
```
we love our blackout night

Blackout Night

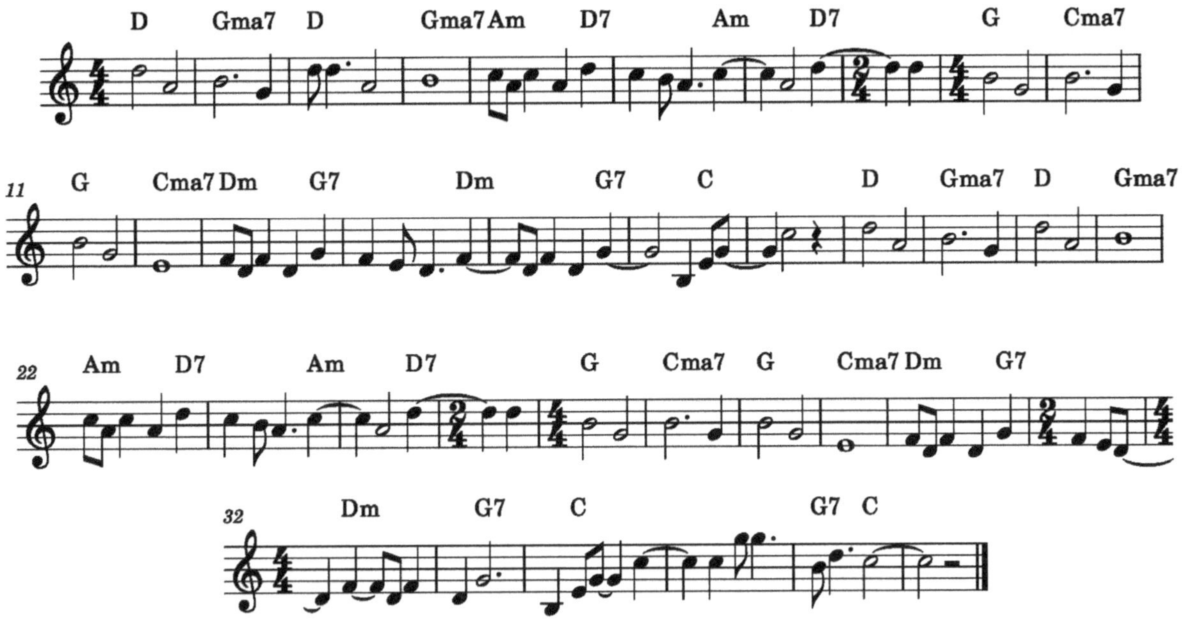

Daisy in the Field

[68 years old . . .]

```
Fma7          C     Fma7          C
once upon a time a long time ago
Dm          G  Dm            G7
nineteen seventy, a boy, he was me
Gma7        D  Gma7             D
once upon a time that boy made a rhyme
Em              A  Em               A7
strumming his guitar, green eyes gazing far
Ama7          E   Ama7              E
that boy was in love with his high school dove
F#m             B    F#m            B7
they shared a mizpah, now she's a grandma
E
he sang . . .
```

[17 years old . . .]

```
Ema9         E   Ema9       E
daisy in the field, lazy after meal
F#m            B   F#m       B7
shining sun on grass, in a photograph
Ema9           E   Ema9            E
Allah paint the sky, colors, lord that fly
F#m           B   F#m           B7      E
I am painter too, when I think of you
```

Daisy in the Field

Imagine That

```
G7   G G7 G                 F          G
what if I bought us that four-room shack?
D             F    D           G       Fma9
what if we get cats, can you just imagine, can you?
G G7   G       F      G
I want you to imagine that


G7    G G7 G              F        G
what if we run off and not look back?
D             F    D           G       Fma9
what if  we get fat, can you just imagine, can you?
G G7   G       F      G
I want you to imagine that


G                     F  G
what if pigs could fly, what if
     Bb              G
politicians spoke the truth?
D                 C7
what if we just smooch?


G7    G G7 G               F         G
what if  I told you right now let's pack?
D             F    D           G       Fma9
what if we did that, can you just imagine, can you?
G G7   G       F      G
I want you to imagine that
```

Imagine That

It's Your Birthday (Uh-huh)

```
D       Dma7    G Gm6                D
happy birthday,  I hope that you're fine
D       Dma7      G Gm6               D       Dma7  A7
happy every day, ah since you've been mine, mine, mine

Dma7 Gma6 Gm Dma7   D
it's your birthday, uh-huh
Dma7 Gma6 Gm   Dma7    D      Dma7 A7
now you're nineteen my love, love, love

D                 Dma7     G Gm6        D
you don't want nothing, ah double negative
D            Dma7       G        Gm6      D   Dma7 A7
but you are everything, my best reason to live, live, live → [it's your . . .]

D       Dma7    G        Gm6      D
let's have Mexican, drink us dos Dos Equis
D           Dma7      G       Gm6      D     Dma7  A7
let's make love again, ah you know it is sweet, sweet, sweet → [it's your . . .]

D      Dma7    G Gm6                D
happy birthday, I know that you're fine
D      Dma7    G      Gm6        D     Dma7 A7
happy everyday till the end of our time, time, time → [it's your . . .]

D                       G            D      A7    G7   G   D
happy birthday, happy birthday, happy birthday to . . . you . . .
```

It's Your Birthday (Uh-huh)

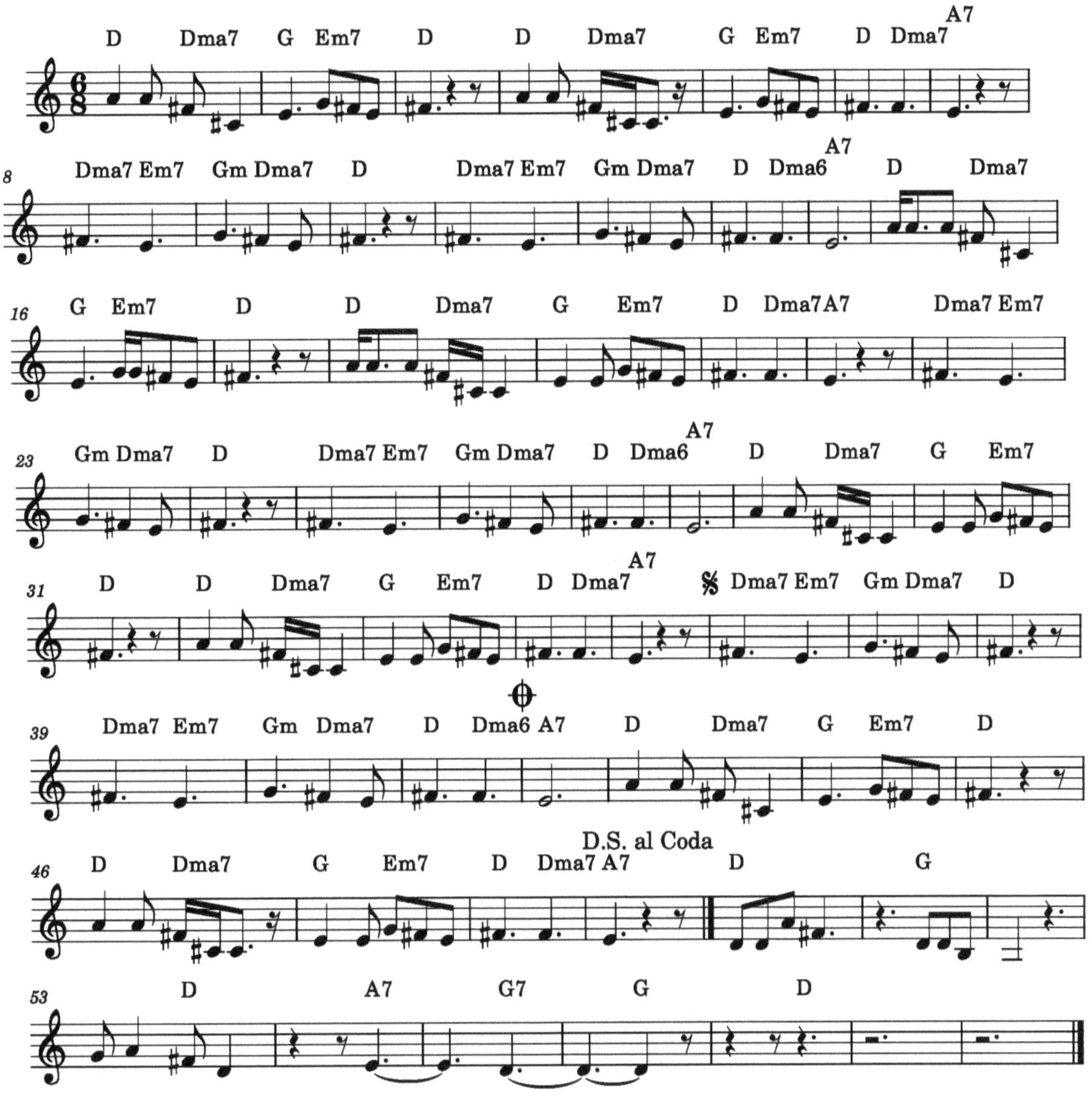

La Vie est Dure

```
E           B7      F#m          Ama7          F#m        B7
```
la vie est dure, she told me, her eyes were gray and sure
```
E           B7        F#m        Ama7      F#m        B7        E
```
I've lived in dreams, I told her I want to meet the queen

```
E           B7      F#m          Ama7          F#m        B7
```
in dreams I flew, she told me but already I knew
```
E           B7      F#m          Ama7          F#m          B7        E
```
it's been so long, I whispered, she kissed me so light and warm

```
Am                        G
```
watching the shadows of St. Charles Avenue
```
F#m                  Ama7
```
rise on the evening walls
```
Am                  G
```
holding a lily, the quiet building
```
F#m                    Ama7                    B7
```
sighs while I sit here watching her wet hair fall

```
E           B7      F#m          Ama7          F#m          B7
```
la vie est étrange, I wondered, the streetcar swayed and lunged
```
E        B7    F#m      Ama7      F#m        B7        E
```
into the dark, the city around me and a billion stars

```
E           B7    F#m          Ama7          F#m        B7
```
la vie est dure, she told me, her eyes were gray and sure
```
E           B7        F#m        Ama7 F#m        B7        E Am E
```
I've lived in dreams, I asked her . . . are you the queen? ah . . .

La Vie est Dure

Oak Trees

```
Cma7                  A        Ama7              D
I asked you to climb oak trees in the park Saturday
Cma7                  A        Ama7              D
part of me wants to hold you, part of me runs away

Cma7                  A        Ama7              D
what's wrong with oak trees? I happen to like them
Cma7                  A        Ama7     D
what's wrong with feelings between friends?

Gma6                     A
I don't know, I hope I never know
Gma6             A        F#7
if I do I'll sure be through . . .

Cma7                  A        Ama7              D
see the touching branches, feel the autumn breeze
Cma7                  A        Ama7                   D
golden sunlight dances, what's wrong with oak trees?

Gma6                     A
I don't know, I hope I never know
Gma6                  A     F#7    Fma7    A
if I do I'll sure be blue . . .
```

Oak Trees

Cma7 A Ama7 D Cma7 A Ama7 D
9 Cma7 A Ama7 D Gma6 A Gma6 A F#7
18 Cma7 A Ama7 D Gma6 A Gma6
25 A F#7 Fma7 A

Sleep with Me

```
Fma9                        G
if I asked you would you sleep with me?
Fma9                        G
if there's a reason not, what would it be?
Dm            D7      Dm              G
it's been three weeks, don't you want to peek?


Fma9                  G
if I told you you are beautiful
Fma9                        G
would you listen to me, would you know
Dm              D7 Dm              G
how it's going to be when you sleep with me?


Fma9                        G
will it feel nice, well now can't you guess?
Fma9                        G
will we get there? yes we will unless
Dm                 D7 Dm          G
you don't want to be in love with me
```

Sleep with Me

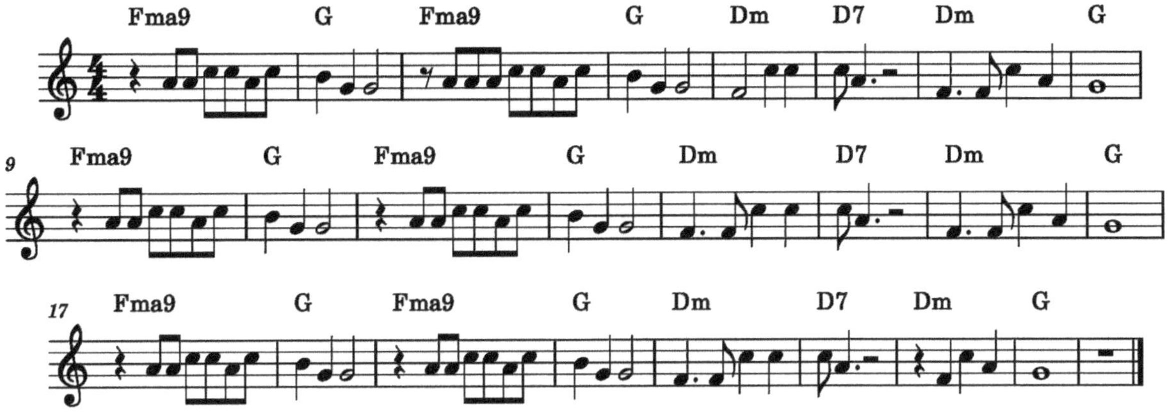

Messing with Me

```
        Gm          Dm      G      D
you're messing with me in a lovely way
Gm        C           D7
how it began I can't say
Gm        Bb          C           D
what is this feeling I'm feeling today?
   Gm          Dm         Gm
so gentle and very much strange
```

```
Gm    Dm             G           D
Twyla knows 'cause you told her, you said
Gm      C            D7
I really fucked with your head
Gm          Bb          C           D
what I want now's to lie down in your bed
    Gm          Dm         Gm
my gentle and very fine friend
```

```
     Gm          Dm      G           D
our phone conversations a soft, soft foreplay
Gm        C           D7
what it all means I can't say
Gm        Bb          C          D
what if I flew up to you this Friday
    Gm   Dm         Gm
for real, for real, to stay?
```

```
        Gm          Dm      G      D
you're messing with me in a lovely way
Gm        C           D7
how it will end I can't say
Gm          Bb          C          D
what if this feeling I'm feeling today
Gm        Dm         Gm      D7   Gm
lasts for all of our days?
```

Messing with Me

Babe of the Blues Bar

```
      Em        G        Cm            Em
the one time I held you we were both high
Em            G        F        Em
shuffling to the blues, a Saturday night
F            Em   Cm            Em
I touched your skin, you . . . let me in


Em             G             Cm             Em
while we were dancing my feelings were mixed
Em          G        F    Em
we were discussing politics
F        Em      Cm          Em
like in a dream, we . . . kept dancing


Em         G              Cm         Em
"One-Eyed Woman" was the name of the song
Em        G        F            Em
I felt your breasts and your cool palms
F            Em   Cm            Em
I touched your skin, you . . . let me in


      Em        G        Cm            Em
the one time I held you we were both high
Em            G        F        Em
shuffling to the blues, a Saturday night
F            Em   Cm            Em
I touched your skin, you . . . let me in
```

Babe of the Blues Bar

This Latest Life

```
Cma7        G                    F G7       Cma7
she believes in many lifetimes, I don't know why
Cma7        G                    F  E7       Ama7
could it be our love was simpler in some past life?
G7          Cma7
well, well, well . . .


Cma7        G                    F  G7    Cma7
I have stood on many beaches, I'm just a man
Cma7     G                  F    E7   Ama7
if I could I'd be the ocean, maybe I am
G7          Cma7
well, well, well . . .


Cma7        G                    F  G7       Cma7
I suppose she had her reasons, we had no ties
Cma7         G                F      E7    Ama7
who knows why she left me in this latest life?
G7          Cma7
well,  well, well . . .
```

This Latest Life

© 1982 David G. Lanoue

Little Green Lizard

```
Am  Asus2 Am  Asus2
Am                D              C        E7
little green lizard you look lost on my window screen
Am                D              F  E7
do you miss the empty lot next door?

Am        D               C          E7
to you I must seem large, a mountain and guitar
Am                D               F  E7   Am  Asus2 Am  Asus2
longing for the happiness we knew

Am                D               C        E7
all you need are dancing weeds, a bug or two
Am          D        F  E7   Am  Asus2 Am  Asus2
she's in Wyoming I heard

Am                   D             C     E7
little green lizard hopping light, I put you outside
Am                D         F  E7 Am
wish it were as easy for me . . .
Am               F  E7      Am  Asus2 Am  Asus2 Am
now you're free . . .
```

Little Green Lizard

© 1982 David G. Lanoue

Real Life

```
       Em              Am      Em          B7
she told me this was real life, not quite a dream
Em    Am    Em      B7        Em
in my room she told me, told me
G                A7    Em        B7   Em
she seemed familiar somehow, I believe


       Em            Am    Em        B7
she knew my situation in just a look
Em        Am     Em    B7            Em
in my confusion I was shook, was I shook
G        A7    Em     B7       Em
when we did it I was, was I, hooked


G    A7    G           A7          Em       B7      Em
real life is not quite a dream, or is it the way it seems?


Em            Am      Em         B7
my house is empty, quiet and bare
Em          Am     Em       B7              Em
she left no traces she was here, was she here?
G       A7   Em         B7            Em
I can't tell, somehow she seems near


G    A7    G           A7          Em       B7      Em
real life is not quite a dream, or is it the way it seems?
G    A7    G           A7          Em       B7    Em
real life is not quite a dream, or is it?
```

Real Life

© 1982 David G. Lanoue

Botanical Gardens

```
C           Cma9 C        D Dadd4 D
something told me when I  got  up
    C     Cma9  C      D   Dadd4 D
I'd find a new way, I had enough
C           Cma9 C        D Dadd4 D
friends expected me to show up
C     Cma9 C   D   Dadd4 D
but I got on a different bus
Fma7       Fma9   G   D  Dadd4 Dma9  D
paid my fare, I saw you on that bus
Fma7  Fma9      G  D Dadd4 Dma9  D
everywhere azaleas, azaleas
```

```
C Cma9  C         D     Dadd4 D
I asked could I walk with you?
C        Cma9  C    D   Dadd4 D
you said yes all in turquoise blue
C     Cma9 C        D    Dadd4 D
by a pond it was  dark and cool
C          Cma9 C      D   Dadd4 D
goldfish floated like big fat jewels
Fma7       Fma9            G  D Dadd4 Dma9  D
walking through the botanical gardens
Fma7       Fma9     G    D  Dadd4 Dma9  D
me and you, my beautiful new friend
```

```
C     Cma9 C     D        Dadd4 D
like a flower you bloomed for me,
C     Cma9 C    D  Dadd4 D
I felt just  like a honey bee
C          Cma9 C   D  Dadd4 D
so drawn to you, felt so  pleased
C          Cma9  C       D    Dadd4 D
Spanish moss hanging in oak trees
Fma7       Fma9            G  D Dadd4 Dma9  D
walking through the botanical gardens
Fma7       Fma9      G    D  Dadd4 Dma9  D
me and you, my beautiful new friend
```

Botanical Gardens

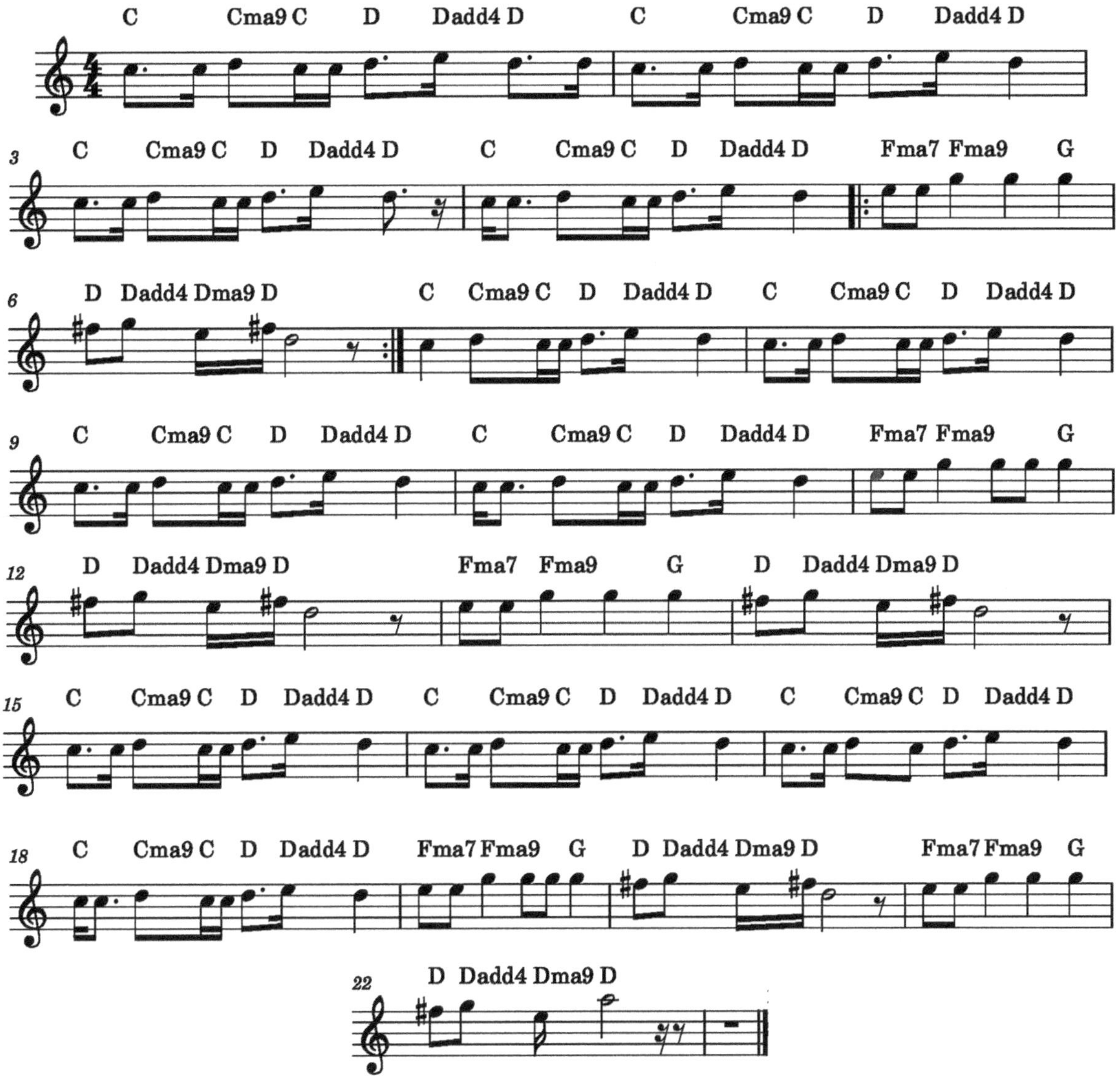

Abby

```
G          Cm                    G
Abby, Abby, won't you please have me?
G          Cm           G
Abby, Abby, why won't you please?
D          C        D        C
I miss you so sadly, I love you so madly
G          Cm           G
Abby, Abby, why won't you please?


D
Abby when we met at school
C
I was such a booking fool
D
Abby when you said your poem
C
in the crowd I felt alone


G          Cm                 G
Abby, Abby, it's been eight years
G          Cm           G
Abby, Abby, I've had six beers
D          C        D           C
I wrote you a letter, I didn't feel much better . . .
G          Cm           G
Abby, Abby, why won't you please?
```

Abby

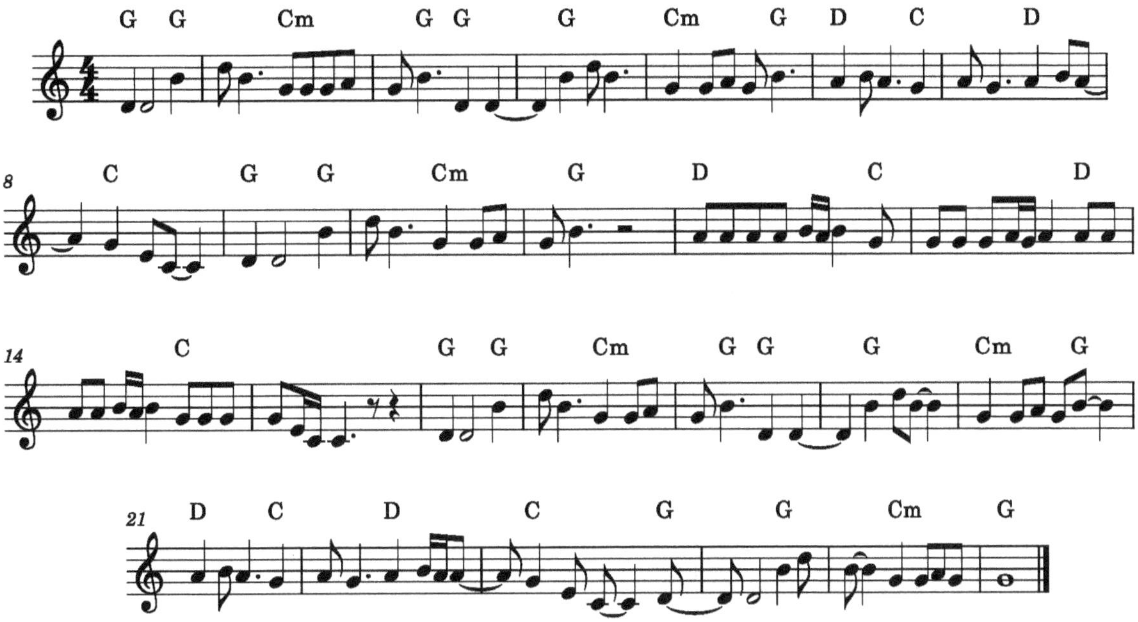

The Summer I Didn't Go to Maine

```
A                         Am6               A
I wrote down all my dreams, maybe that sounds strange
 A                        Am6           A
I bought designer jeans, guess I needed a change
    E       D    D7   A
the summer I didn't go to Maine
    E       D          D7        A
the summer I stayed in the New Orleans rain


     A                    Am6                  A
she came by every day, I knew what she was thinking of
        A                    Am6         A
we'd put on the Lionel Richie tape, lay down, make love
    E       D    D7   A
the summer I didn't go to Maine
    E       D   D7   A
the summer I fell in love again


     A                    Am6            A
we sat out on the Moonwalk watching ships flow by
   A                            Am6     A
we laughed a while and talked, I got lost in her eyes
    E       D    D7   A
the summer I didn't go to Maine
    E       D   D7   A
the summer I let her slip away


  A                          Am6             A
I wonder what it's like up there in a lighthouse by the waves
A                          Am6              A
though I didn't go nowhere, guess it evens out someway
    E       D    D7   A
the summer I didn't go to Maine
    E       D          D7        A
the summer I stayed in the New Orleans rain
```

The Summer I Didn't Go to Maine

© 1984 David G. Lanoue

Joanie

```
A              G    C        G
Joanie sailed to sea, I stayed on the land
A              G    C        G
she looked for me, I hadn't the time
A        G    C        G
all I could do was wave goodbye
A              G        C        G        A
she turned her head, the wind became dead for Joanie

        Bb           F        C        Bb           F
when sea turned to land the flowers left the hand of Joanie
Bb         F                C        Bb                      F
yesterday someone said they saw her, they weren't sure, oh no

D7
she left her popo, her ma and her dad
G7                C7
thinkin' about the fun she would have . . .
D7
she left her boyfriend, her job and her school
G7                      C7           A
her membership to the private pool, Joanie

A         G        C              G        A
once in a while my brain paints her smile, oh yeah
A         G    C        G    A
now and then I hope that she is high
                        G    C        G        A
'cause if she drowns in that sea because of me I would die
```

→ [Joanie sailed to sea . . .]

Joanie

Ghost

```
A                        Dm
she walks by my window on a rainy morning
G            A     Dm
I've just seen a ghost, blowing past my window
E7          A   Bm
I want her so, dressed in black
E7                        A
from her head to her toes . . .


A                                Dm
nights have been too dreamless, days are filled with meanness
G       A    Dm
I'm all alone, going through the motions
E7           A       Bm
my heart is stone, under an umbrella
E7          A
I want her so . . .


A               Dm
she is a stranger, must be a neighbor
G       A    Dm
I've never seen, blowing past my window
E7            A       Bm
I'm having a dream, dressed in black
E7                  A
as she's vanishing . . . gone
```

Ghost

A Dm G A Dm E7 A
7 Bm E7 A A Dm
13 G A Dm E7 A Bm E7 A
20 A Dm G A Dm E7 A
27 Bm E7 A

© 1982 David G. Lanoue

Easton

```
E                              G#add5
Easton, before you change the world
E                              A7
seein' that you're that kind of girl
G#add5                              F#7
when you build your dreams up to the clouds
G#add5                         F#7
please remember what I tell you now
             E    B7        A    E
build balconies, Easton, for me


E                              G#add5
Easton, the kind of architect
E                   A7
even a poet can respect
   G#add5                              F#7
so when you build your dreams up to the clouds
G#add5                         F#7
please remember what I tell you now
             E   B7               A    E
build balconies, Easton, remember me


E                              G#add5
Easton, do you like the birds?
    E                         A7
the meaning in between my words?
   G#add5                              F#7
and when you're standing up there in your clouds
G#add5                    F#7
visionary sunrise, I see you now
             E   B7     A           E
on a balcony, Easton, you and me
```

Easton

Mine All Mine

```
Ema9          C#m          A7    D
```
every time I look at you, and I do
```
Dma9        C#m      E
```
look at you all the time
```
Ema9             C#m          A7        D
```
I'm astounded, I'm in shock, because you
```
Dma9        C#m      E7
```
chose to be mine all mine

```
          Fma7    Em
```
life is a gift
```
Gma7      F#m
```
love is a bliss
```
Ema9      C#m      A7
```
everyone doesn't find, so

```
Ema9          C#m          A7    D
```
every time I look at you, and I do
```
Dma9        C#m      E
```
look at you all the time
```
Ema9             C#m          A7        D
```
I'm astounded, I'm in shock, because you
```
Dma9          D    E7  A
```
chose to be mine all mine

Mine All Mine

Mingling Dust

```
D          G#dim     Gm        D
```
I want to hold you all night long
```
D          G#dim Gdim          D
```
until the rosy, soft light of dawn
```
D          G#dim     Gm          D
```
I plan to love you till you must leave
```
D              G#dim Gm              D
```
I'll keep your ashes where mine will be
```
D     G    Gdim        D
```
lucky us, mingling dust

```
D                  G#dim   Gm        D
```
when our two bodies, so close, sing
```
D                  G#dim     Gdim        D
```
stardust with stardust, light shimmering
```
D                  G#dim   Gm      D
```
someday they'll pour us into a sea
```
D          G#dim     Gm      D
```
there I will love you eternally
```
D     G    Gdim        D
```
lucky us, mingling dust

Mingling Dust

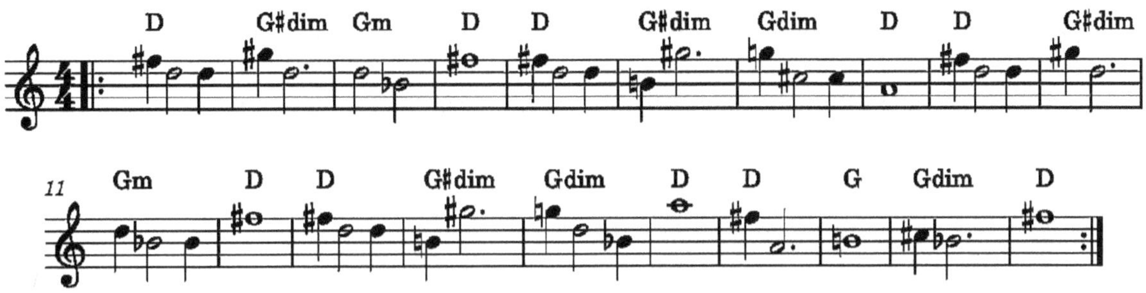

Knit One Purl Nine

```
F                                Am
yarn ball of iridescent pink, there's no need to think
Bb   C    C7    F
knit one, purl nine
F                                         Am
whole world's going down the drain, thieves control the game
Bb   C    C7    F
knit one, purl nine
C                      Em           G7
making a sweater, feels so much better
```

```
F                                Am
headlines screaming on your phone, you don't cry, don't moan
Bb   C    C7    F
knit one, purl nine
F                                Am
pretty grandma stitching a surprise for a young child's eyes
Bb   C    C7    F
knit one, purl nine
C                      Em           G7
making a blanket, someday you'll thank it
```

```
F                          Am
outside a pitter-patter rain, hatred, lies and pain
          Bb   C    C7    F
but you knit one, purl nine
F                          Am
yarn ball of duck-egg blue, you just being you
Bb   C    C7    F
knit one, purl nine
C                      Em        G7
making a present, feels so pleasant
```

```
F                          Am
yarn ball of iridescent pink, there's no need to think
Bb   C    C7    F
knit one, purl nine
```

Knit One Purl Nine

© 2019 David G. Lanoue

Back with You

D D D D D D D

```
G                                          D
back with you, ooo yes I'm where I belong
A         G    D                   G
ooo you're finally mine yeah, hurting is through
      D
cuz I'm back with you

G                                          D
back with you, ooo yes I'm where I belong
A         G    D                   G
ooo you're finally mine yeah, starting like new
      D
cuz I'm back with you


D7                    D7
so much between us, no one could see us
D7
we couldn't be us, but our love freed us

G                                          D
back with you, ooo yes I'm where I belong
A         G    D                   G
ooo you're finally mine yeah, hurting is through
      D             G      D
cuz I'm back with you, yes I'm back with you
G         D
yes I'm back . . . with . . . you
```

Back with You

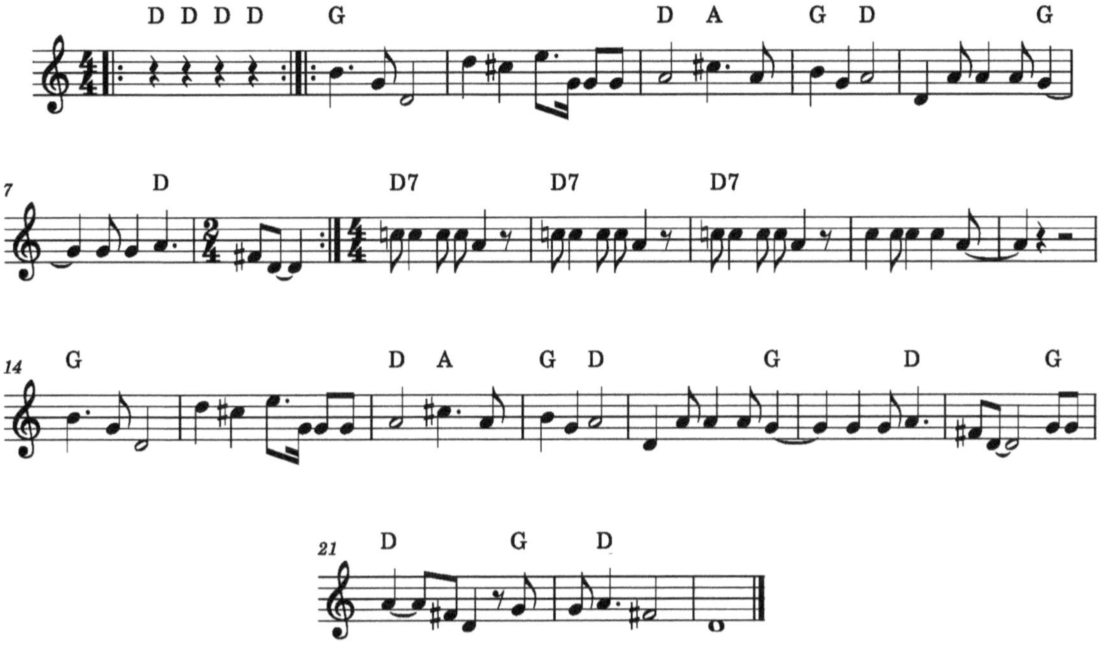

African Princess

```
    Am    G          Am        C    A7
my African princess with wild ocean hair
      Am        Em      G    E7
your fierce eyes beyond compare
Am        G          Am          C    A7
day starts to darken, the moon in the west
    Am    G    E7
my African princess


    Am    G          Am              C    A7
my African princess with smooth shining skin
      Am      Em    G    E7
our life once again begins
Am          G      Am          C    A7
night starts to deepen, come, we will rest
      Am      G    E7      Am
my African  princess
```

African Princess

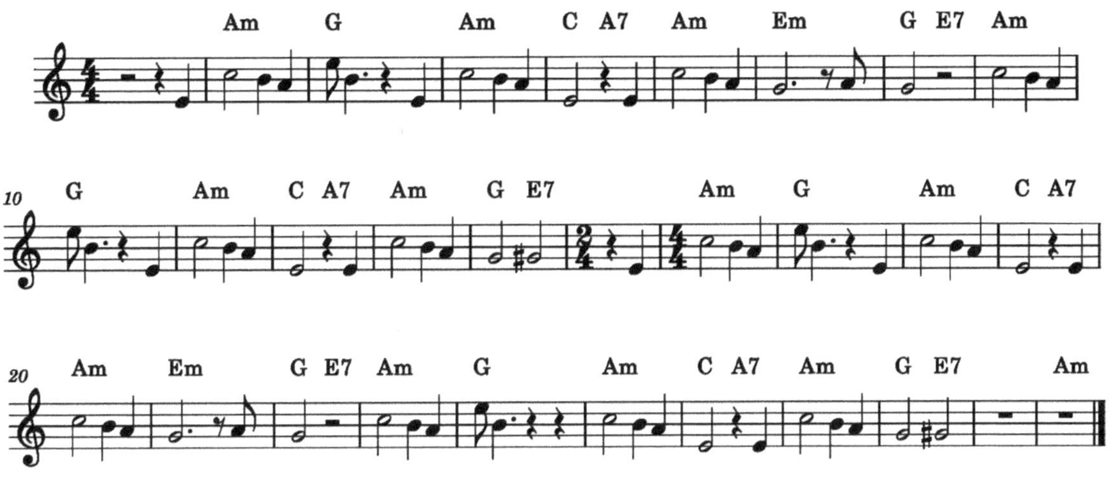

© 1985 David G. Lanoue

Dreaming the Moon

```
Bm                      G
dreaming the moon, thinking of you
Bm                   G
wondering who you are
 Bm               G
alone in the night, I'm locked in tight
Bm                      G
one window bright with stars
A          G          Bm
and I want to dream the moon
A          G          Bm
I just want to dream the moon


Bm                 G
tired of the bars, counting the cars
Bm                      G
out there it's dark and deep
Bm            G
and will it last? that's all I ask
Bm               G
I should be fast asleep
A          G          Bm
but I want to dream the moon
A          G          Bm
I just want to dream the moon


Bm                 G
it's been a while without your smile
Bm                   G
touch me and I'll be free
Bm                      G
dreaming the moon, thinking of you
Bm               G    A
wondering who are we
A          G          Bm
and I want to dream the moon
A          G          Bm
I just want to dream the moon
```

Dreaming the Moon

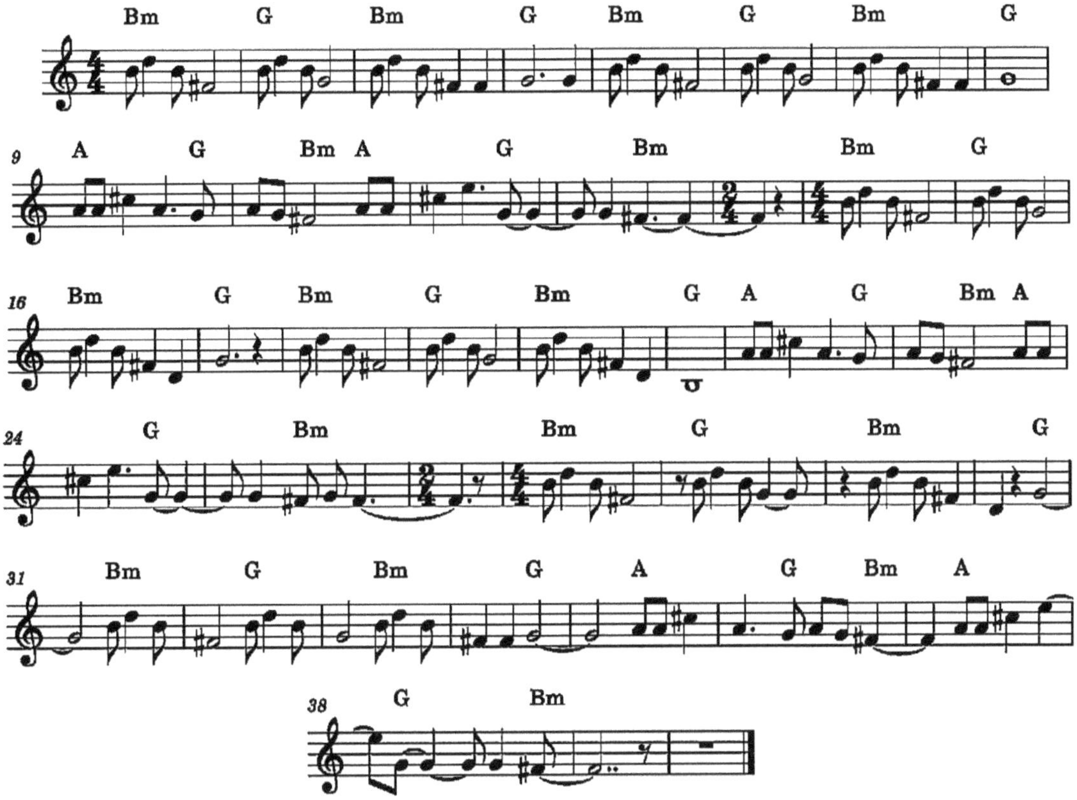

© 1984 David G. Lanoue

One Foot in the Grave

```
Bm                       F#m
one foot in the grave, I went on a date
Am                   Bm   Bbm
held your little hand too late
Am                   Em
maybe should've hid a ring on a plate
G                Am  Gm
with a silver lid, too late

Gm                Dm
Yumi, you and I crossed horns with fate
Fm                Gm  F#m
we kissed our kiss too late
Fm                   Cm
high in Kyoto Tower the champagne was great
D#                Fm       Em
I gave you a flower too damn late
Em         Bm        D       Em
too damn too damn too damn late
```

One Foot in the Grave

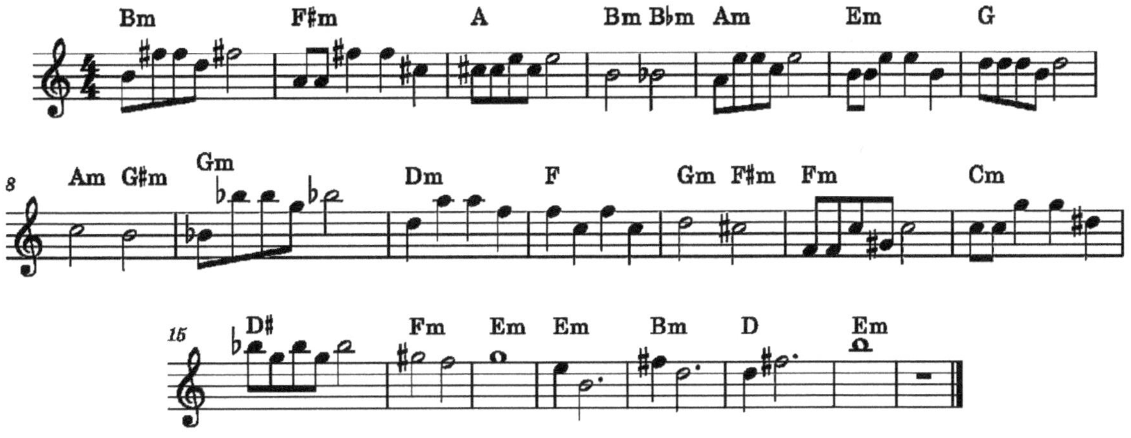

I Lose Touch with Reality

```
F                 C    F            G7
I lose touch with reality, far too much I daydream
F             C   G    F       G   F G7
when I want to say things I'm too late, so late
```

```
F          C    G    F            G7
I don't study at my desk, I like muddy days the best
F        C    G    F          G7
so I walk into the rain, I know I go insane sometimes
F          G    F            G7
finding I'm too late, finding I'm too late
```

```
C     Am      Dm     F    F         Dm        F     G
I can't write for money, love, poems to make days sunny, love
F                        Am
far too much I wander in the rain
F                        G7
far too much I wander in the rain, the rain and
```

```
F                 C    F              G7
I lose touch with reality, cannot find you baby
F             C   G    F       G   F G7   C
when I want to say things I'm too late, so late
```

I Lose Touch with Reality

© 1970 David G. Lanoue

Nowever

```
C     Cma9    D   D7
forty years ago
C   Cma9 D     D7
my wild time
C   Cma9     D    D7
I'm pouring wine
C     Cma9  D  D7
on a balcony


C   Cma9   D     D7
pretty new friend
C       Cma9 D     D7
bright afternoon
C   Cma9     D      D7
I forget your name
C   Cma9    D7
but not our kiss


C     Cma9   D  D7
forty years ago
C Cma9 D   D7
I  visit still
C   Cma9 D   D7
that balcony
C   Cma9 D7
that afternoon


E                Em6
blue spinning sky
E        F#7
without end
A        Am
now is forever
     D7          E
my pretty new friend
```

102

Nowever

New Normal

```
Fma7           C            Fma7        Gdim
```
she's my new normal, our dress quite informal
```
        Fma7        G            C
```
on our date to the movie in the den
```
Fma7           C            Fma7        Gdim
```
intimate pandemic, our love quite hygienic
```
        Fma7        G                C
```
as we dine on the grub Grubhub sends

```
      C           E          A           B7
```
we used to go places, we used to see faces, in
```
Fma7          G7           C
```
places where whole faces were
```
      E          A          B7         Fma7
```
but then every nation on pandem-vacation
```
   G7             Fma7         G
```
the world became just me and her

```
Fma7           C            Fma7        Gdim
```
teaching our classes, the laddies and lasses
```
        Fma7        G            C
```
in our dress-up pajamas with no socks
```
Fma7           C            Fma7        Gdim
```
still we keep on eating with masks on and greeting
```
        Fma7        G            C
```
Instacart and the Blue Apron box

```
      C           E          A           B7
```
we used to go places, we used to see faces, in
```
Fma7          G7           C
```
places where whole faces were
```
      E          A          B7         Fma7
```
but then every nation on pandem-vacation
```
   G7             Fma7         G
```
the world became just me and her → [she's my new normal . . .]

New Normal

Heart-shaped Food

```
        D              Am
don't tell me it's no good
C              D
heart-shaped food
G                        Dm
pork chops show a tender mood
F            G
heart-shaped food
    C7                      Bb        D
spaghetti pierced with an arrow of asparagus


D                    Am
Valentine Day's no joke
C         D
pass the artichokes
G                        Dm
omelet sizzling just to please
F            G
gooey-hot cheese
C7           Bb                   D
after dinner, we'll guess Victoria's secret


        D              Am
don't tell me it's no good
C              D
heart-shaped food
G                        Dm
pork chops show a tender mood
F            G
heart-shaped food
    C7                      Bb        D
spaghetti pierced with an arrow of asparagus
```

Heart-shaped Food

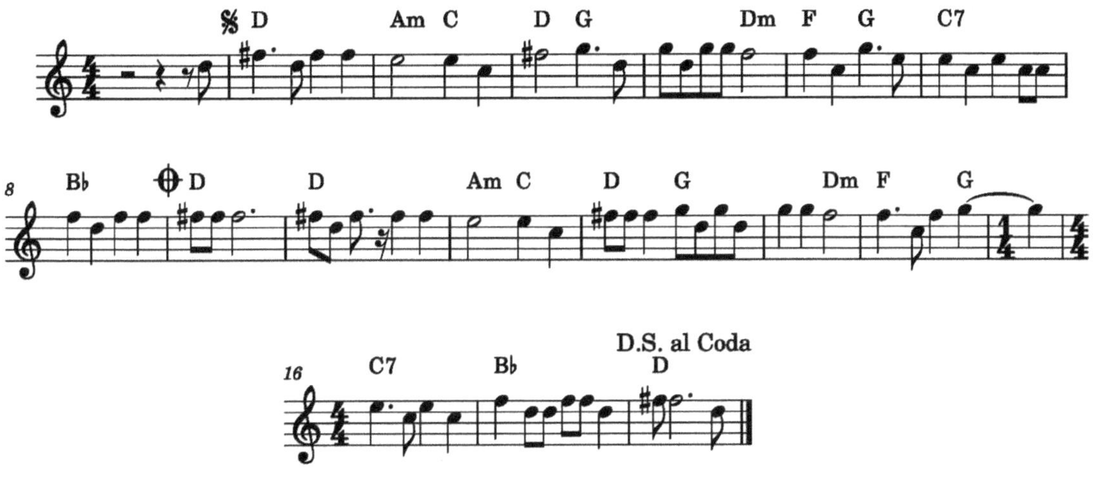

© 2022 David G. Lanoue

Oscar the Ferret

```
E   B7      Dm6 Am      E                      B7
Oscar the ferret had fleas, scratched on trees
        E      Am        E              B7    E
and he loved it, he could bend, my little furry friend

E     B7         Dm6 Am       E            B7
saw him in the pet store, all alone, sisters sold,
        E           Am        E            B7        E
and he looked so bored, poor Oscar, come home with me

E      B7    Dm6  Am         E                B7
we became partners, everywhere people'd stare
            E  Am        E              B7        E
at me and Oscar on my arm, my little good luck charm

E           B7   Dm6 Am      E            B7
he walked like a slinky, so alert, he loved dirt
            E     Am   E       B7           E
and slept with me, so sweetly curled at my feet

E             B7  Dm6    Am        E                 B7
the good die young and this is true for ferrets too
        E    Am         E            B7        E
when I held him that last time, he never closed his eyes

E  B7        Dm6  Am          E            B7
if there's a heaven and somehow I'm allowed
    E   Am         E              B7    E
to get in I'll see Oscar, my little furry friend
```

Oscar the Ferret

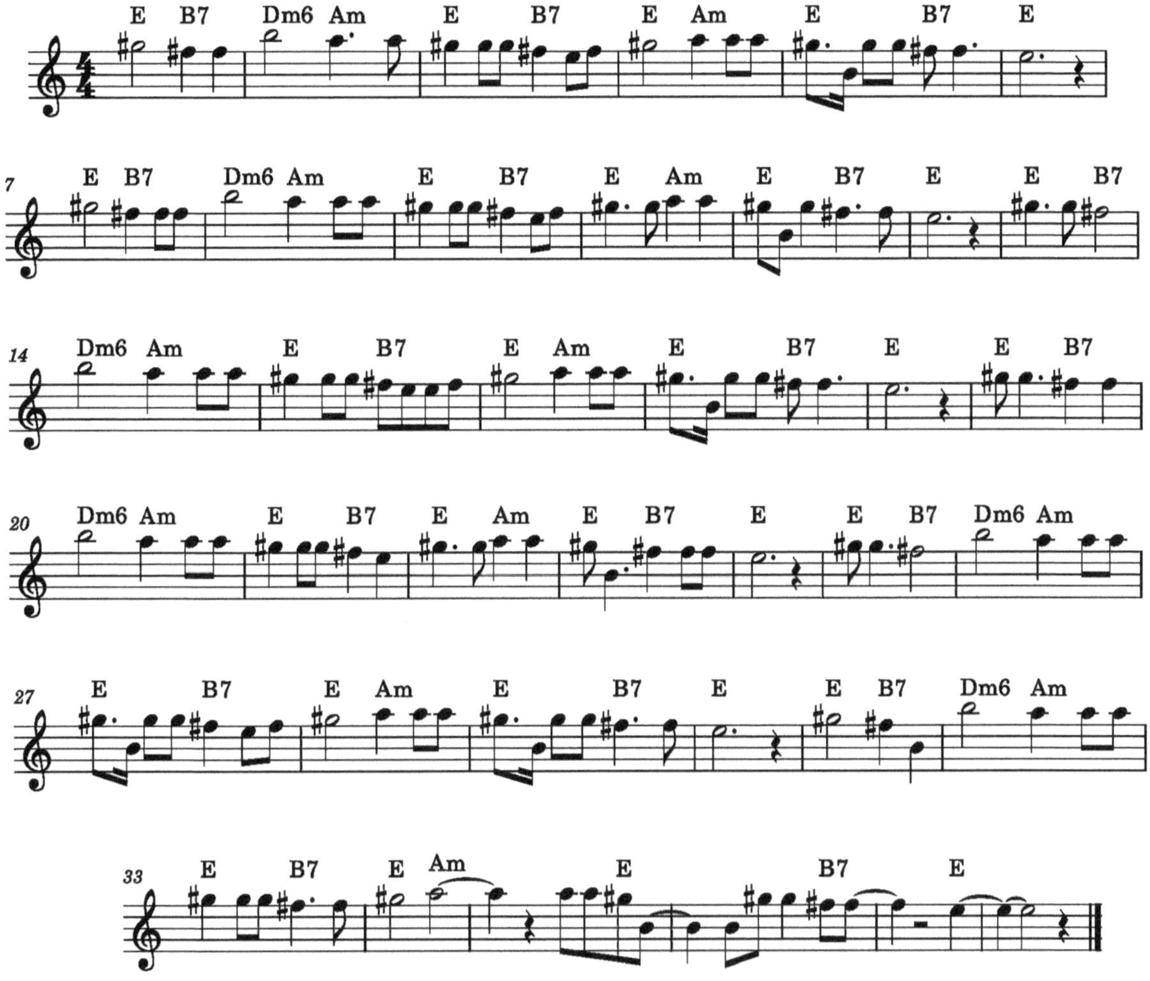

Be My Girl

```
Cma7                Gma6      Cma7                    Gma6
I learnt the law of laughter, I walked on roads of pain
Cma7              Gma6  Cma7                 Gma6
but I survived disaster just long enough to say


A          Fma9
be my girl
A          Gma6
be my girl
A               Fma9        Cma7  Gma6
you are the world . . . to . . . me . . .


Cma7                Gma6      Cma7                    Gma6
I learnt the law of women, I messed my share of minds
Cma7              Gma6  Cma7                 Gma6
I hope it's all forgiven, I'm tired of my old lines → [be my girl . . .]


Cma7                Gma6      Cma7                    Gma6
I learnt the law of violence, just hiding in my room
Cma7                Gma6    Cma7                 Gma6
the loaded guns of silence, I've had it with that gloom → [be my girl . . .]


Cma7                Gma6  Cma7                 Gma6
I learnt the law of Jesus, was kneeling at my pew
Cma7                Gma6   Cma7                      Gma6
I chewed that host to pieces, what else was there to do? → [be my girl . . .]


Cma7                Gma6  Cma7                 Gma6
I learnt the law of music, just swaying with that moon
Cma7              Gma6    Cma7                 Gma6
I watched a gory sunset, I ate my last mushroom → [be my girl . . .]


Cma7                    Gma6  Cma7                 Gma6
we learn the laws of the Maker, we practice one or two
Cma7                Gma6      Cma7                      Gma6
but we are born lawbreakers, they can't keep me from you → [be my girl . . .]
```

Be My Girl

Changed

```
E            Dma9        A           Ama9
some days I wake up, I don't know why
E            Dma9        A
seems like my whole life's changed
E            Dma9     A          Ama9
I'm peeking out at a dark early sky
E            Dma9        A
I'm feeling high and strange
            E  Bm6  Am6        E  Bm6  Am6
high and strange . . .   I have changed . . .


E            Dma9            A           Ama9
over the telephone she says, "Hey you!"
          E            Dma9        A
she's cocked like a hot handgun
E            Dma9               A           Ama9
I should be hanging up, should think things through
E            Dma9        A
I should turn around and run
A          E  Bm6  Am6              E  Bm6  Am6
I should run . . .      but that ain't fun . . .


E            Dma9        A         Ama9
how to explain the things I do
E            Dma9        A
can't lose, I can't quite win
E            Dma9            A           Ama9
she is a door marked, "Stay out fool!"
E            Dma9        A
why am I pushing in?
A                E  Bm6  Am6          E  Bm6  Am6              E  Bm6  Am6
I'm pushing in . . .      I can't win . . .        I should run . . .
                  E
but that ain't fun . . .   → [some days I wake up . . .]
A          E  Bm6  Am6                E
I should run . . .      but that ain't fun . . .
        E
I have changed again
```

Changed

Coincidence

```
D                     Em      A7           Bm
missed my bus that Sunday, so I went the other way
   D              Em   A7        D
in turquoise blue a lady, I saw her eyes
   D                  Gm       C              Bm
if not for the Big Shot root beer I would never have met her
D                  Em      A7      D
I would never have let her tell me lies


   D                  Em  A7          D
coincidence pickin' on me with a capital C
D              Em        A7       Bm
I'm down on my knees, coincidentally
D     Em   A7        D    D   Em   A7          D
la la la la la-la-la-la, la la, la la la la la-la-la-la la, la, la


   D                    Em       A7            Bm
we strolled the botanical gardens, felt my fantasy harden
D                 Em        A7       D
down in pond's cool bottom goldfish dived
D                Gm        C             Bm
pretty soon I had her number, she had me way under
D             Em        A7       D
her soft kiss a wonder, I felt alive → [coincidence pickin' on me]


D                 Em   A7                Bm
now it's one year after all that mid-March laughter
D              Em        A7       D
I thought I would have her all my own
    D                 Gm           C             Bm
but she wasn't free, he caught her, a lost lamb to the slaughter
D                   Em      A7   D
looking down in the water, I'm alone → [coincidence pickin' on me]
```

Coincidence

Conversational

```
    E                    Ama7
"Do you love me?" "Yes I do."
  Ema9 E     A    Ama7 Ema9 E     A     Ama7 D7
"Well then show me. Can you show me how?"
    E                    Ama7
"How I love you!" "No you don't
Ema9 E    A    Ama7 Ema9 E   A  Ama7 D7
cuz you hurt me." "But I'm sorry now."


    E     D Dma9 D  D7
how I do love you
Ema9   D7               E
I can't prove . . . but I do


    E                    Ama7
"There's temptation all around
Ema9 E  A Ama7 Ema9 E  A   Ama7 D7
this old city, fine and pretty ones,
 E                    Ama7
fast flirtations . . ." "They don't count!"
 Ema9 E     A    Ama7    Ema9 E  A  Ama7 D7
"But they hurt me." "And I'm sorry now." → [how I do love you . . .]


    E                    Ama7
"Do you love me?" "Yes I do."
 Ema9  E    A    Ama7 Ema9 E   A     Ama7 D7
"But you said these exact words before."
 E                    Ama7
"That was different." "No it's not."
Ema9 E    A          Ama7
"But I've changed now.
Ema9 E    A   Ama7 D7
can't we try once more?" → [how I do love you . . .]
```

Conversational

Gerard and Natasha

Em   C
see the girl, she's a mystery, she is all alone on New Year's Eve
      A7
she is holding on but it's so hard to breathe
B7
why can't they just let her be?

Em
see the boy on the green futon
          C
getting tired of looking at the silent phone
       A7
he is holding on but it's so hard alone
     B7
he wonders why she doesn't come

Em   C   B7
if you're wondering who these two might be
              Em   C   A7
they're Gerard and Natasha, Gerard and Natasha, Gerard and Natasha
   B7   Em
Gerard and Nata . . . sha

Em
see the girl, she's in her killer car
      C
on the High-Rise gliding underneath the stars
      A7
she is happy now but what she did was hard
B7
hard to make a brand-new start

Em   C
see the boy, he opens up the door, she is standing there and her
                   A7
eyes are sure, the futon flopping open on the floor
B7
she's the one he's waited for → [if you're wondering . . .]

118

Gerard and Natasha

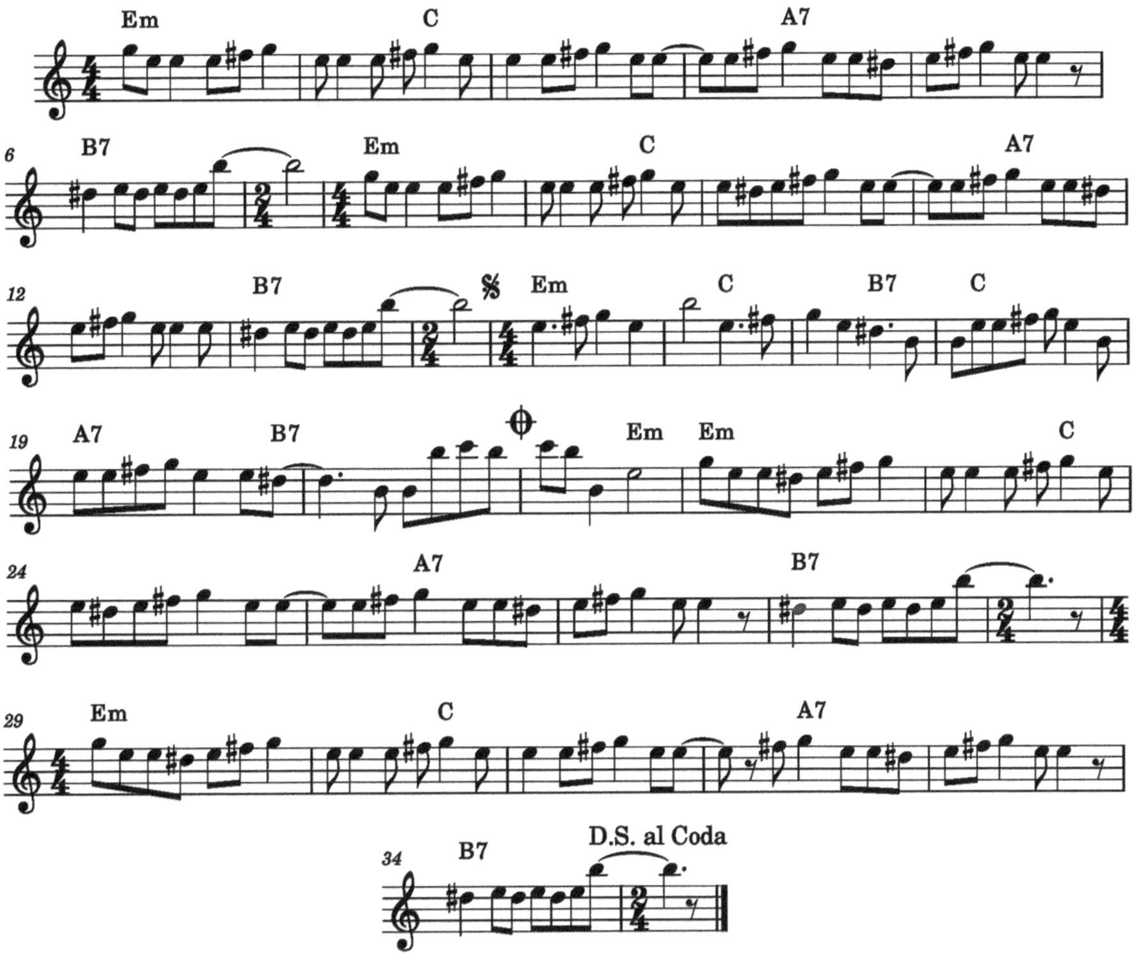

Give It to Me

```
Em              D                 Em
give it to me, I never had it so good, ooo
A7
not till you
G               A7            Em
I said never, I mean never, had it so good
```

```
Em              D                     Em
tell it to me, I never heard such sweet lies, ooo
A7
not till you
G               A7            Em
I said never, I mean never, heard such sweet lies
```

```
Em            D          C           A7        Em
give me what nobody, nobody ever gave . . . to me
```

[instrumental verse]

```
Em              D             Em
listen to me, I never felt it so deep, ooo
A7
deep in you
G               A7             Em
I said never, I mean never, felt it so deep  → [give me what . . .]
```

Give It to Me

I Wandered Through the Mardi Gras

```
    Am                                      F
I wandered through the Mardi Gras, I cannot tell you what I saw
   G        Am                                      F
I saw what I saw, no question in my mind, I'm in love but listen I
G            Am        Fm6      Gm6        Am          Am
don't know what for, what for, what for, I don't know what for
Am                              F
there's a woman in my dreams, I lost her once or twice it seems
   G        Am                              F
I did what I did, no question in my mind, I'm in love but listen I
G            Am        Fm6      Gm6        Am          Am
don't know who with, who with, who with, I don't know who with
     Am                          F
my life's a gaudy big parade with roaring clowns in masquerade
   G        Am                                      F
I catch what they throw, these strangers in disguise with plastic faces with no
                                                            [eyes
   G            Am        Fm6      Gm6        Am          Am
I want what they know, they know, they know, I know they know
Am                              F
there's a woman in the crowd, she thinks like me, she looks around
     G            Am                              F
she sees what she sees, no question in her heart, she's in love and looking
                                                            [hard, she's
G            Am    Fm6      Gm6        Am        Am
looking for me, for me, for me, looking hard for me
Am                              F
after all the crowds are gone, clean-up trucks roll in the dawn
G        Am                              F
spraying a mist, no question in my mind, I'm in love but listen I
G            Am        Fm6      Gm6        Am
don't know who with, who with, who with, I don't know who with
```

I Wandered through the Mardi Gras

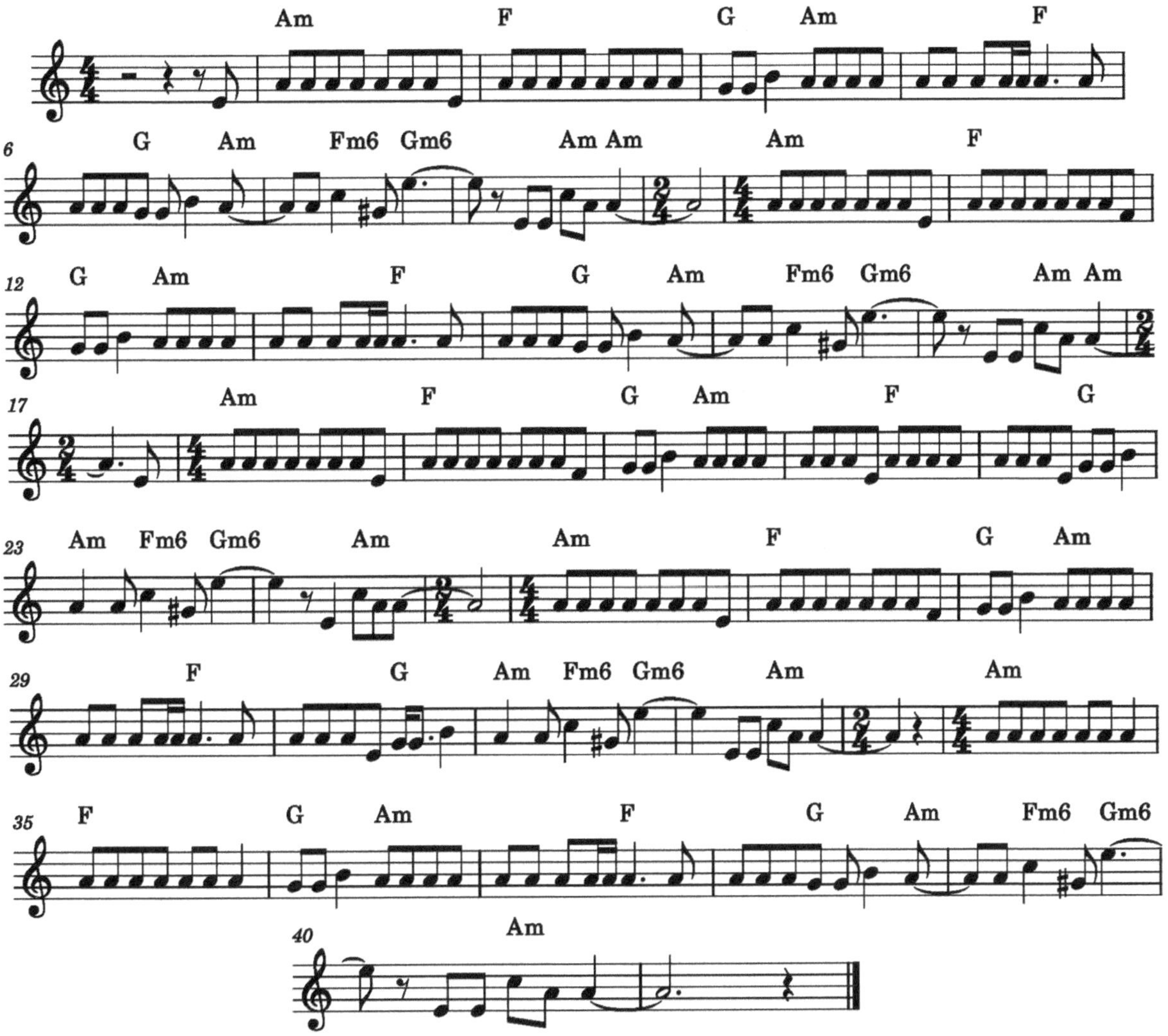

© 1984 David G. Lanoue

I Won't Marry Your Mother

```
G           E7        C           D7   G        E7   C  D7  G
childhood is hard for a little girl who plays alone in the yard
G           E7            C           D7          G        E7   C  D7
mother knows best and her little girl like a slave in her pink party dress
G           E7       C         D7       G        E7   C  D7
always in control, the years for this little girl slowly unfold
G           E7            C       D7    G
finally on her own, but the past is a heavy stone


G                       E7
girl, I'll love you like no other,
      C     D7         G
but I won't marry your mother


G                         E7          C               D7   G        E7   C  D7
why do we fight and fuss, stupid little things destroy  our basic trust
G                     E7          C         D7            G
words we don't mean fly, my father's anger, your mother's cold reply


G                       E7
girl, I'll love you like no other,
      C     D7         G
but I won't marry your mother
```

I Won't Marry Your Mother

Cousin Linda

E
she lives in a house
     D   A   E
and all the big people stand around her
    E
she looks in the mirror
        D   A   E
and the beauty of earth surrounds her
     B7   A   E   B7 E
in my mind, and she always shines in darkness

E
she lives in my heart
     D   A   E
and rides the big people in the rain
    E
she plays the piano
     D   A   E
and stars fall down to spell her name
     B7   A   E   B7 E
and I know, that she always shines in darkness

E
she lives in a dream
     D   A   E
and cries for my mind to set her free
          E
she puts on a silver ring
     D   A   E
and I know that my eyes cannot see
     B7   A   E   B7 E
for the light, cuz she always shines in darkness

Cousin Linda

© 1969 David G. Lanoue

Morning Glory

```
Ema9                              C           D
there is a road inside you and I know you're on it
Ema9                              G    A
maybe it leads to my room, girl I really want it
Ema9                              C     D       E
come see the morning glory growing in my head for you


Ema9                              C           D
there are so many questions and I know you've asked them
Ema9                              G      A
images and sensations that I know you bask in
Ema9                              C     D       E
don't miss the morning glory growing in my head for you


E   Ema9  D    F#7
morning glory growin'
E      Ema9 D     F#7
that's my story, woman


Ema9                          C D
maybe it's not your karma, baby, to love me
Ema9                              G      A
maybe I'm not the partner, woman, that you seek
Ema9                              C     D       E
but I have a morning glory growing in my head for you


E   Ema9  D    F#7
morning glory growin'
E      Ema9 D     F#7
that's my story, woman


Ema9                              C           D
there is a road inside you and I know you're on it
Ema9                              G    A
maybe it leads to my room, girl I really want it
Ema9                              C     D       E
come see the morning glory growing in my head for you
```

Morning Glory

Shit or Get Off the Toilet

```
E                         A                 E
shit or get off the toilet, that's what they say
E                             F#m       B7
a wedding ring won't spoil it, I think I'll stay
E                         A             E
if we don't do this now we might slip apart, let's
A             E   F#m             A     E
shit or get off the toilet, you . . . own my heart


E                           A               E
I called the place your work, I heard your sweet voice
E                               F#m           B7
that guy you live with's a jerk, he won't bring you joy
E                         A           E
you sobbed into the phone, I said I love you, it's time to
A             E   F#m         A     E
shit or get off the toilet, say . . . our I do's


E                             A               E
we're only twelve years late but better late than never
E                             F#m     B7
who else loves you this way? we're birds of a feather
E                         A             E
last night inside a dream I kissed your soft mouth, why don't we
A             E   F#m         A     E
shit or get off the toilet? let's marry now
```

Shit or Get Off the Toilet

© 1997 David G. Lanoue

Miss Mexico

```
Badd4                     Ema9
look at us just kicking up the sand
Badd4                     Ema9
it was summer, we had lovely plans
F#m        Adim  F#m     Adim     A
I took your hand down in Tuxpan Mexico
```

```
Badd4                           Ema9
our loose muffler rattled in the square
Badd4                            Ema9
you posed by the statues we found there
F#m        Adim  F#m       Adim        A
stone matadors, mine and yours, Miss Mexico
```

```
Em          F#7      Em  Adim A
how you glowed, my Miss Mexico
```

```
Badd4                           Ema9
look at us just scarfing down the food
Badd4                        Ema9
all night on the toilet feeling crude
F#m         Adim F#m      Adim     A
but we had fun down in Tuxpan Mexico
```

```
Badd4                           Ema9
waking up in that strange dark hotel
Badd4                           Ema9
watching you asleep and then I felt
F#m         Adim F#m     Adim         A
like a matador, forever yours, Miss Mexico
```

```
Em          F#7    Em  Adim  A
now you know, my Miss Mexico
```

Miss Mexico

I Like Her

```
C                              Am
she's smooth as the sheets in a convent
C                          Am
funny like the lies of the president
        C                          Am
she's real like a breeze with an unknown scent
        C                    Am
she's right as a kiss you really meant


 C          Am        C          Am
I like her, she likes me, I like her, she likes me
 C              Am C         Am        C
I like her, she likes me and that's alright,
Am
that's alright


        C                        Am
she's whole as the soul in a loaf of bread
C                            Am
easy as a song playing in your head
        C                        Am
she's light as a pea on a featherbed
        C                      Am
she's right as a word you wish you said → ["I like her . . ."]


        C                        Am
she's free like the dream of a butterfly
C                            Am
sweet as the ooze in a cherry pie
        C                          Am
she's strange like fish falling from the sky
        C                  Am
she's ripe as a jewel in a baby's eye → ["I like her . . ."]


   C
alright
```

I Like Her

© 1984 David G. Lanoue

New Songs

```
D              A          C          G
tried making a tape for you, I thought that I could
D              A          C          G          D
played all of my old, old songs, but it wasn't good, it wasn't good

D              A          C          G
Suzanne, what you do to me, you know that it's true
D              A          C          G          D
can't play how I used to be cuz you made me new, now I'm new and it's

D   A   C     G
new songs I want to sing for you, that
D   A  C     G          D
new joy I want to bring to you, new

D              A          C          G
had my fair share of sadness, I think that you know
D              A          C          G          D
heartbreak and that loneliness, I'm letting it go, letting it go

make way for those → [new songs . . .]

D              A          C          G
now I'm flying to see you, we won't be the same
D              A          C          G          D
we're starting all over fresh, Suzanne is the name I can blame

for those → [new songs . . .]

D      C     G   D  C     G
cuz I'm brand new, I'm brand new
D      C     G
and so are you
```

136

New Songs

Me and You

```
     G
she waits at the bus stop all alone
     Gm          C7   G
her mind is flying in the sky
     G
the rain has drenched her to the bone
        Gm        C7      G
but the sky is blue and she's dry
      D           C    D    C
she got a fortune cookie yesterday
D         C   D          C                    G
and in her ears the words still play hey hey hey hey hey!

       G              C                    G
you'll find a friend to love you, singing it's me and you
  G         C                    G    C     D    D7
a crazy boy, a lazy boy, singing it's me and you, me and you

G
the bus pulls up, the brakes do groan
     Gm             C7   G
her mind's still flying in the sky
     G
she gets in the backseat all alone
       Gm            C7   G
in the midst of friends who sigh
      D           C    D    C
she met her fortune cookie yesterday
D        C   D         C                  G
and in her ears his words still play hey hey hey hey hey! →[you'll find . . .]

         G
me and you . . .
```

138

Me and You

G Gm C7 G G
8 G Gm C7 G G D C D
16 C D C D C G G C
24 G G C G C D D7 G
33 Gm C7 G G
40 Gm C7 G D.S. al Coda D7 G

© 1973 David G. Lanoue

Our First Kiss

```
      E                   F#7
her dad was a dentist, Mom wore perfume
A                   E       Ema7 Fdim E
she splashed some on too for our first kiss


      E                     F#7
the braces she wore all silvery wires
A           E         Ema7 Fdim E
I tasted her fire during our first kiss


E                   F#7
it was dead winter, I walked her home
A               E         Ema7 Fdim E
we stopped in the snow for our first kiss


E                 F#7
icy wind blowing, I felt her need
    A                   E       Ema7 Fdim E
so warm pressed against me for our first kiss


E                       F#7
all these years later, wherever she lives
        A               E       Ema7 Fdim E
does she remember the bliss of our first kiss?
```

Our First Kiss

Ruby Type "E"

```
Dm              C7        Dm
see the girl in her thrift shop
Dm            Bb7 C7   Dm
what a world she has got
Dm                    C7      Dm
eyes that shine with far-off light
Dm          Bb7   C7 Dm
into mine, what a sight


Dm  Bb7   C7    Dm    C7       Dm
that Ruby type "E," oh Ruby, Ruby


Dm               C7    Dm
see them go onto Desire
Dm           Bb7 C7 Dm
buy it low, sell it higher
Dm                    C7       Dm
full-length mirrors so she can dance
Dm           Bb7 C7 Dm
no more fears, in a trance


Dm  Bb7   C7    Dm    C7       Dm
that Ruby type "E," oh Ruby, Ruby
```

["E" for excellent, she claimed]

Ruby Type "E"

Stepping Off Together

```
              E                 Bma6  A                    E
I never felt so stepping off together, but now I do
              E                 Bma6   A                   E    A7  E
I never felt like getting lost forever like I do with you
```

```
     Fma7                         C
my family doesn't know what it is
Fma9                        Am
strangers don't know what it is
Bma6                  A
why won't they let us live? → [I never felt . . .]
```

```
Fma7                      C
now you're afraid it will end
Fma9                  Am
how can I say it won't end?
Bma6            A
will you be my friend? → [I never felt . . .]
```

Stepping Off Together

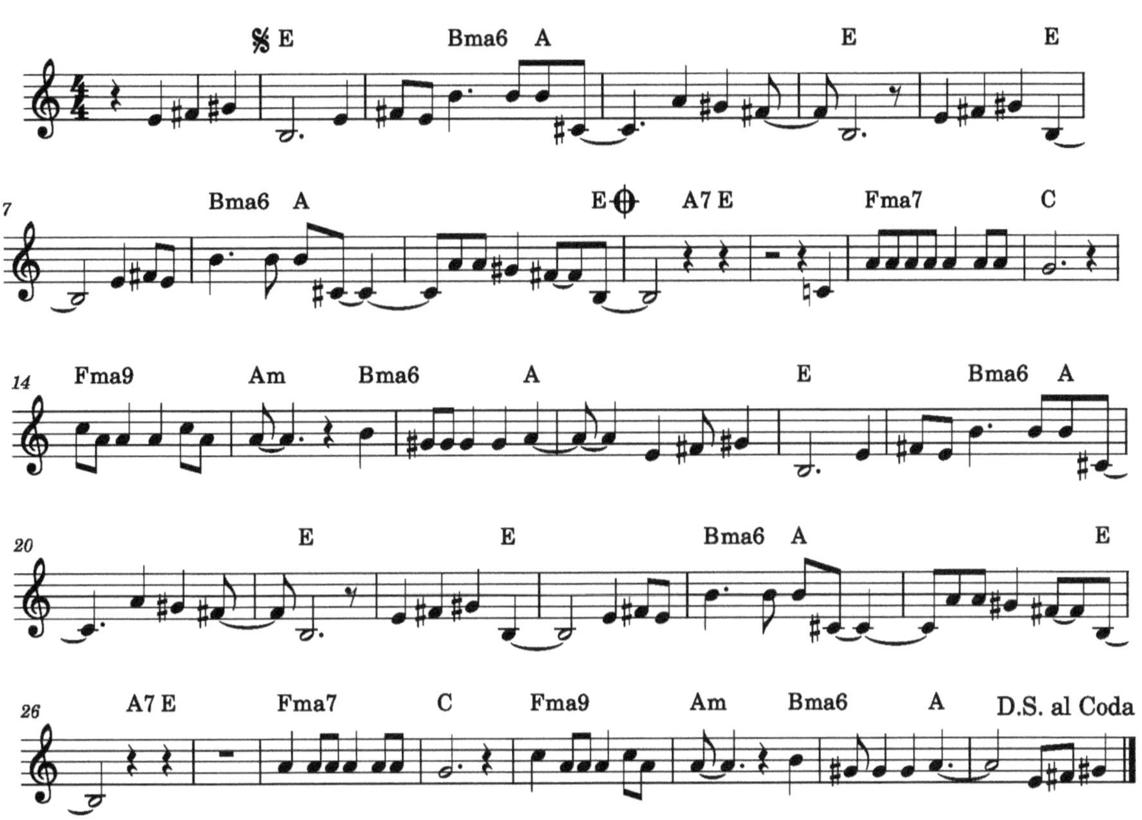

The Love That Never Happened

```
E               Am          E           Em6
thank you for the love that never happened
      E           Am6     E   Bm6
have a good ride to Dallas today
E               Am          E           Em6
thank you for the smiles I used to bask in, still do
E               Am6             E
thank you thank you thank you, thank you


E               Am          E           Em6
bless you for your care, I did without it
      E           Am6         E   Bm6
have a good life with happiness inside
E               Am          E           Em6
bless you for your kiss, I dreamed about it, still do
E               Am6             E
bless you bless you bless you, bless you


  E             Am        E           Em6
I loved though our love never happened
        E           Am6     E   Bm6
it was good knowing you for a while
  E             Am            E           Em6
I loved though I stayed in the background, still do
E               Am6             E
loved you loved you loved you, I loved you


E               Am          E           Em6
thank you for the love that never happened
        E           Am6     E   Bm6
have a good ride to Dallas today
E               Am          E           Em6
thank you for the smiles I used to bask in, still do
E               Am6             E
thank you thank you thank you, thank you
```

The Love That Never Happened

147

What a Person Loves

```
G              Em            Bm
when I saw you standing in the sky
     G               Em           Bm
your cloud-hair falls, you rain, I start to cry
G            Em           Bm
when I saw your eyes were seeing me
G              Em              Bm
once I was blind but now it's plain to see


         E            Bm
what a person loves is beautiful
     E          A        Cma6  D7  Cma6  D7
and beautiful is what you are . . .


G            Em              Bm
now I see you shake your head at me
     G              Em         Bm
but what one loves is truth, reality
G          Em            Bm
now I think I'll fall, I'll rain, I'll cry
       G              Em            Bm
it's so good to be wet because I was so dry


         E            Bm
what a person loves is beautiful
     E          A        Cma6  D7  Cma6  D7  G
and beautiful is what you are . . .
```

What a Person Loves

© 1972 David G. Lanoue

When the World is a Can of Schlitz

Em6 . . .
```
              C          Am    Em            F#7
when the world is a can of Schlitz in your hand
        A         F#m     F     E     Em6
and you feel like recyclable aluminum
                C          Am        Em            F#7
when the woman you want has a drawer full of men
        A         F#m         F        E     Em6
and she flips you her Kodachrome album of them
```

```
           F#7  G    A         G
what's the use? you can't compete
        A            F#m           F           G           C
you just need, you just need, you just need, you just need . . . that girl
```

```
Am   Em   F#7   A   F#m   F   E   Em6
```

```
              C            Am   Em            F#7
when committees without pity hang you to dry
          A       F#m           F        E     Em6
and you're left there twisting on your best necktie
              C          Am    Em         F#7
when the woman you love belongs to the spa
     A          F#m             F           E     Em6
surrounded by musclemen with bad-ass red cars → [what's the use . . .]
```

```
             C            Am              Em          F#7
when you've done all you could and you've got your degree
        A       F#m         F              E     Em6
you're filling the bathtub to do your laundry
             C          Am           Em            F#7
when the woman you crave has them lined to the sea
          A          F#m                  F              E        Em6
and they canceled your credit cards, you're down on your knees
```

```
                    C
→ [what's the use . . .]
```

When the World is a Can of Schlitz

151

Why Do I Wonder?

```
Dm                             E7                        A7 Dm
I see truth in your wide eyes, in the rain we kiss goodbye . . .
Dm                             E7                        A7 Dm
won't see you till Saturday, we agree it has to be this way . . . then

Dm         C         Dm     C
why do I wonder? why if I know how you feel?
Dm         C                           Dm
why do I wonder (and I wonder) if it's real?

Dm                             E7                        A7            Dm
in my room it's night again, 12-inch TV you're my faithful friend . . . oh . . .
Dm                             E7
out there in the city night, somewhere safe I hope
        A7     Dm
she's alright . . . but → [why do I . . .]

Dm                             E7                        A7            Dm
I see rain or is it tears? making love but are you really here? I don't know
Dm                             E7                   A7    Dm
your umbrella floats away, I watch you fading into gray . . . and

→ [why do I . . .]
```

Why Do I Wonder?

© 1985 David G. Lanoue

High-Rise Girl

```
C                    Em          Fma7
high-rise girl, she knows what I need
C       Em F    C       Em    Fma7 C
if I only believe, if I only could believe
Am      G7          C    G7
and she lives on the other side
Am      G7        C
my girl from the East


C                      Em        Fma7
high-rise girl, she's not in the least
C                Em F
someone I could release
C            Em Fma7
I could never
   C    C+      Fm      G#7
release, please, please, please!
C      G7       C
my girl from the East
```

High-Rise Girl

© 1986 David G. Lanoue

I'm Your Pillow

```
D          Dma7    G      A              D
when you're ready for sleepy time, I'm your pillow
D          Dma7    G            A         D
when you're weary because you're mine, I'm your pillow
D7    G         A  Ama9 D7    G          A      Ama9
I'm your pillow for REMs, I'm your pillow cuz we are friends
D7    G         A          Ama9            D
I'm your pillow, our love won't end, I'm your pillow


D          Dma7        G      A              D
when you've finished your mint ice cream, I'm your pillow
D          Dma7    G      A            D
when you're ready to catch a dream, I'm your pillow
D7    G             A      Ama9 D7    G            A          Ama9
I'm your pillow when we're in bed, I'm your pillow when books are read
D7    G         A      Ama9            D
I'm your pillow to rest your head, I'm your pillow


         D      Dma7      G      A            D
when we wake up and the day is new, I'm your pillow
D      Dma7   G      A          D
you hold me and I hold you, I'm your pillow
D7    G             A      Ama9 D7      G            A      Ama9
I'm your pillow in the rising sun, I'm your pillow till the coffee comes
D7    G             A      Ama9          D
I'm your pillow while we cuddle some, I'm your pillow
```

I'm Your Pillow

157

Lonely Cricket

```
E            C+    Cma9  D   C         C+      E
I'm a lonely cricket in the dark singing my cricket song
E         C     Cma9      D
will I ever finally make my mark
   F#7      Gma6        E7
or do all my notes sound wrong?


E            C+    Cma9  D   C             C+ E
I'm a lonely cricket in my hole, wings are my violin
E            C      Cma9      D
rock n' roll or country, hip-hop, soul
     F#7          Gma6  E7
I'm begging for love again


G#        C+      Fm        C+
cricket so lonely, staying up late
G#        C+      E7
cricket so low and blue
G#         C+      Fm        C+
crickets, we signal, crickets, we wait
G#         C+      C7
crickets, we need love too


E            C+    Cma9  D   C         C+      E
I'm a lonely cricket at the pub trying out my new line
E            C      Cma9      D
girl, your pretty neck deserves a rub
   F#7      Gma6        E7
I bet I can guess your sign      → ["cricket so lonely . . ."]


     G#
we do!
```

Lonely Cricket

© 2023 David G. Lanoue

Robots

```
Dm                       G
I fell in love with a robot
G7         A7              D
she's got such a lovely smile
Dm                          G
I don't have to tell you that she's hot
Em6         Dm6            D
I've sought her for quite a while
Am     D          D7   E7      A7
robot toy, I'm a robot boy, oh joy!


Dm             G
we're biological robots
G7         A7                D
we've got well-programmed brains
Dm                          G
we evolved, now we have fresh thoughts
Em6     Dm6           D
robots kissing in the rain
Am       D          D7         E7        A7
two machines, we know what it means to love!


Dm               G
I fell in love with a robot
G7         A7              D
she's got such a lovely smile
Dm                            G
I don't have to tell you that she's hot
Em6         Dm6            D
I've sought her for quite a while
Am     D          D7         E7        A7
two machines, we know what it means to love . . .
         D
robot love!
```

Robots

Dm G G7 A7 D Dm G Em6 Dm6
7 D Am D D7 E7 A7 Dm G G7 A7 D Dm
15 G Em6 Dm6 D Am D D7 E7 A7 Dm
22 G G7 A7 D Dm G Em6 Dm6 D Am D
29 D7 E7 A7 A7 D

Slow Down/Go Down

```
G         Dm6        C         G
we went down to the Audubon Zoo
G    Dm6       C      G
all alone in the tropical room
G    Dm6        C          G
I was happy, our love it was new
G          Dm6    C           G
turning to go my mouth found you, I said

G                                    C  Cma9 G
slow down slow down slow down slow down . . .
G                                    C  Cma9 G
we said go down go down go down go down . . .

G         Dm6     C        G
birds of paradise hid in the green
G    Dm6     C          G
I was waking from a long dream
G    Dm6     C        G
softly talking, gurgling stream
G          Dm6  C          G
bright little ducks waddled and preened, they said → [slow down . . .]
```

Slow Down/Go Down

Wish I

```
D      Dadd4     D       Dadd4  D
wish I knew the answer when I see her
Bb         D
and she asks me
Dadd4  D           Dadd4 D
oh, she needs me to console her
Bb         D       Dadd4      D
take her sorrow, break her pain oh
Bb    D            Bb         D
but I don't know,  but I don't know . . .


D      Dadd4        D         Dadd4        D
wish I knew where dreams flow, down what mountain
Bb         D
to what meadow
Dadd4 D        Dadd4  D
and I need her to console me
Bb         D       Dadd4      D
take my sorrow, break my pain oh
Bb    D            Bb         D
but I don't know, but I don't know . . .
```

Wish I

© 1971 David G. Lanoue

Wonder Bread

```
D              Dma9
you are Wonder Bread, you build strong
C           Cma9
bodies twelve ways
D           Dma9   G
I need you all my days
C                Cma9        Bb
you are Wheaties, breakfast of champions
Bbma9
my love
C                Cma9       D
you are Wonder Bread for me


D              Dma9
I'm in good hands, you are All State
C           Cma9
you make me whole
D              Dma9   G
you're my Spaghetti-O's
C                Cma9        Bb
you are Wheaties, breakfast of champions
Bbma9
my love
C                Cma9       D
you are Wonder Bread for me


F         Fma9     G   G7
you're the best commercial
F       Fma9    C
for not being alone
F       Fma9   G   G7
it's not controversial
D       Dma9            G7
I'm the dog, you're Milk-Bone → [you are Wonder . . .]
```

Wonder Bread

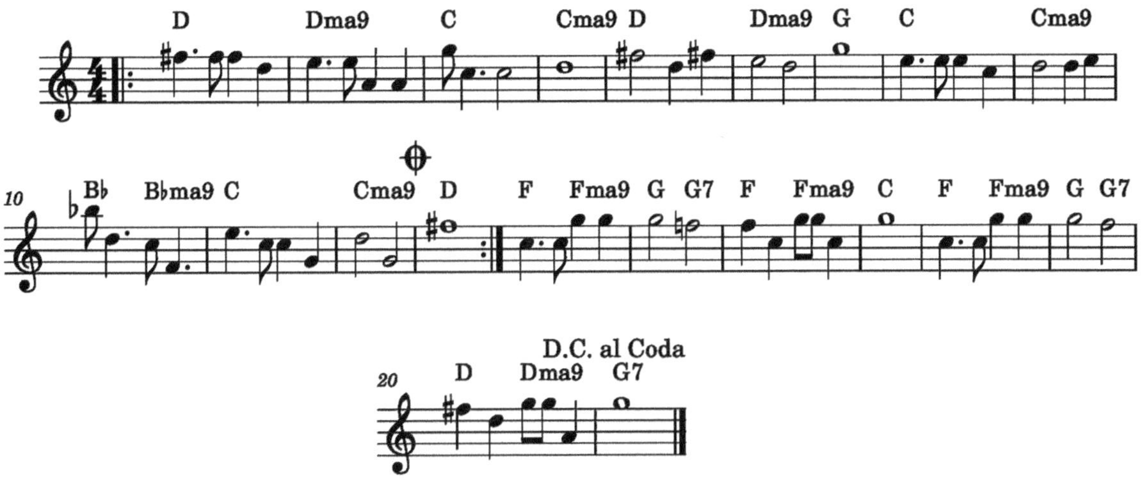

I'm Here

```
Fma7                          E
```
thanks for the frozen enchiladas
```
Fma7                     Ema9
```
six packs of El Cheapo beer
```
Fma7                          E
```
though I don't say this too often
```
Ema9  F#7  Fma7      E
```
I . . . . 'm here

```
Fma7                          E
```
don't want to take you for granted
```
Fma7                          Ema9
```
though we've been lovers half a year
```
Fma7                          E
```
don't want to let you feel abandoned
```
Ema9  F#7  Fma7      E
```
I . . . . 'm here

```
Fma7                          E
```
thanks for all those stolen pizzas
```
Fma7                          Ema9
```
I-love-you's breathed in my ear
```
Fma7                          E
```
though I'm selfish I still need ya
```
Ema9  F#7  Fma7      E
```
I . . . . 'm here

I'm Here

Got My World

```
    Bm                    E
I see you in an office sitting by a window
A           E
the sun shines in
      Bm                       E
you look just like an artist cramming Chemistry
A        E    G     D  E   G  D  E
I have to grin, have to grin


        Bm                 E
we're sitting in a movie sharing popcorn
A           E
searching for clues
    Bm                         E
I think you are so soothing on my futon
A           E    G   D     E   G  D  E
reading the news, reading the news


        Bm                 E
it's like the day I told you, I told you
A           E
I love you girl
        Bm                    E
and every time I hold you, I hold you
A           E    G   D  E   G  D  E
I've got my world, got my world


        Bm                      E
and now you're making pizzas in the East, yeah
A           E
I miss you bad
Bm                           E
and when I finally see ya, I'll see ya
A        E    G  D  E   G  D  E
I'll be so glad, be so glad        just → [like the day . . .]
```

170

Got My World

© 1986 David G. Lanoue

Temple of Three Pines

Ama9 A   A A   G7
In a temple of three pines
Gma6   A   Gma6   A
on our backs, looking up
Ama9 A   A   A   G7
I decided you are mine
Gma6 A   Gma6   A
on a blanket, side by side

Ama9   A   A   A G7
we saw seagulls, kites so high
Gma6 A Gma6 A
radio playing low
Ama9   A   A   A   G7
sad old opera, hours passed by
Gma6   A   Gma6 A
and the sun in the sky

Ama9 A   A A   G7
in a temple of three pines
Gma6   A Gma6   A
you and me, us made three
Ama9 A   A   A G7
and I told you, you're so fine
Gma6   A   Gma6 A
and you smiled in reply

Temple of Three Pines

173

We Won

```
C                Adim
I will hold you close
Dm                    G7
till you fall in the golden sun
C                Adim
you loved me the most
F             C#7       C
more than anyone has done


E          Gdim
golden sun
Am       D7   G#7  G7
race is run, we won


C                Adim
if they're keeping score
Dm                    G7
though we met so late in the game
C                    Adim
we have shared much more
F             C#7          C
than what many lovers can claim  → [golden sun . . .]


C                Adim
I will hold you close
Dm                    G7
till you fall in the golden sun
C                    Adim
you loved me the most
F             C#7       C
more than anyone, we won


E          Gdim
golden sun
Am       D7   G#7  C
race is run, we won
```

We Won

CHORDS USED IN THIS BOOK

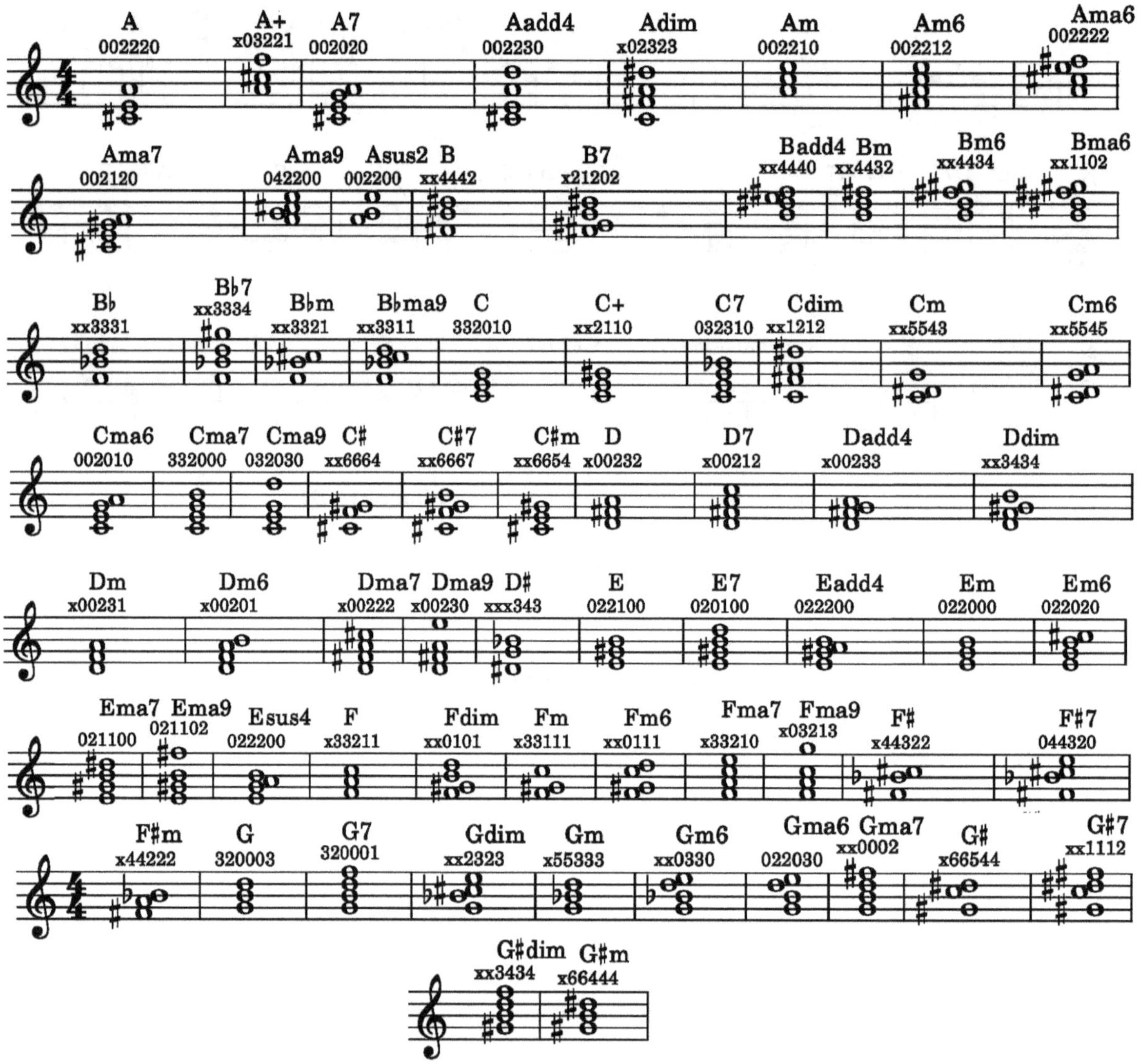